First published by Brockhampton Press Ltd
20 Bloomsbury Street
London WC1B 3QA

© Brockhampton Press Ltd, 1997
© Lys de Bray (all illustrations and original text), 1997
© Savitri Books (this adaptation and layout), 1997

ISBN 1-86019-416-8

Printed and bound in Italy

The quotations from William Shakespeare
used in this book have been taken from
The Temple Shakespeare, Cambridge edition,
printed by J. M. Dent in 1895.

ELIZABETHAN GARLANDS

Lys de Bray

BROCKHAMPTON PRESS

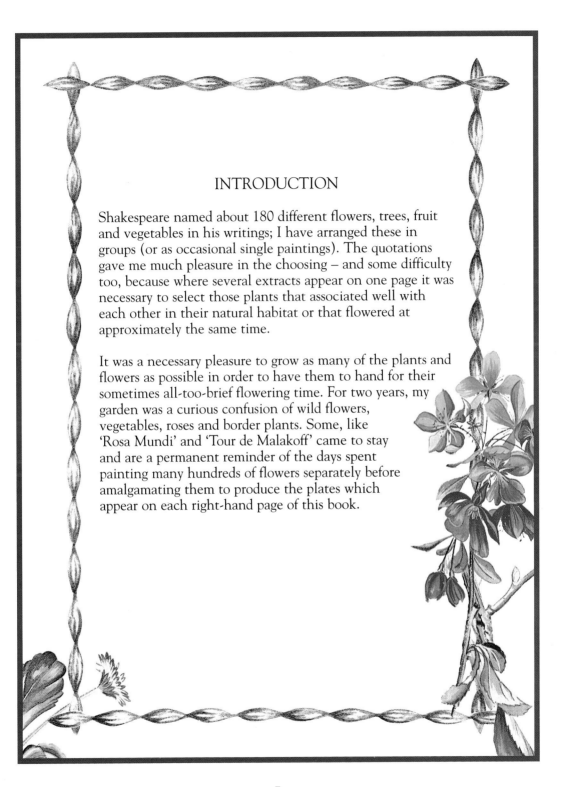

INTRODUCTION

Shakespeare named about 180 different flowers, trees, fruit and vegetables in his writings; I have arranged these in groups (or as occasional single paintings). The quotations gave me much pleasure in the choosing – and some difficulty too, because where several extracts appear on one page it was necessary to select those plants that associated well with each other in their natural habitat or that flowered at approximately the same time.

It was a necessary pleasure to grow as many of the plants and flowers as possible in order to have them to hand for their sometimes all-too-brief flowering time. For two years, my garden was a curious confusion of wild flowers, vegetables, roses and border plants. Some, like 'Rosa Mundi' and 'Tour de Malakoff' came to stay and are a permanent reminder of the days spent painting many hundreds of flowers separately before amalgamating them to produce the plates which appear on each right-hand page of this book.

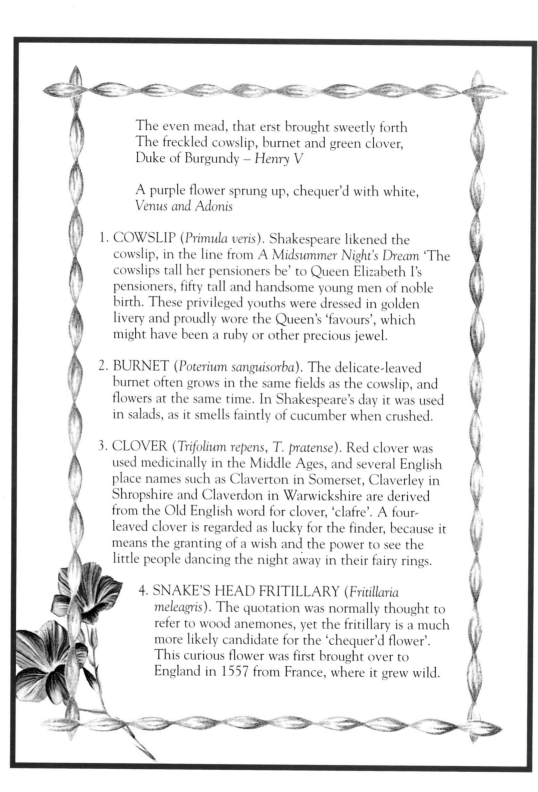

The even mead, that erst brought sweetly forth
The freckled cowslip, burnet and green clover,
Duke of Burgundy – *Henry V*

A purple flower sprung up, chequer'd with white,
Venus and Adonis

1. COWSLIP (*Primula veris*). Shakespeare likened the cowslip, in the line from *A Midsummer Night's Dream* 'The cowslips tall her pensioners be' to Queen Elizabeth I's pensioners, fifty tall and handsome young men of noble birth. These privileged youths were dressed in golden livery and proudly wore the Queen's 'favours', which might have been a ruby or other precious jewel.

2. BURNET (*Poterium sanguisorba*). The delicate-leaved burnet often grows in the same fields as the cowslip, and flowers at the same time. In Shakespeare's day it was used in salads, as it smells faintly of cucumber when crushed.

3. CLOVER (*Trifolium repens, T. pratense*). Red clover was used medicinally in the Middle Ages, and several English place names such as Claverton in Somerset, Claverley in Shropshire and Claverdon in Warwickshire are derived from the Old English word for clover, 'clafre'. A four-leaved clover is regarded as lucky for the finder, because it means the granting of a wish and the power to see the little people dancing the night away in their fairy rings.

4. SNAKE'S HEAD FRITILLARY (*Fritillaria meleagris*). The quotation was normally thought to refer to wood anemones, yet the fritillary is a much more likely candidate for the 'chequer'd flower'. This curious flower was first brought over to England in 1557 from France, where it grew wild.

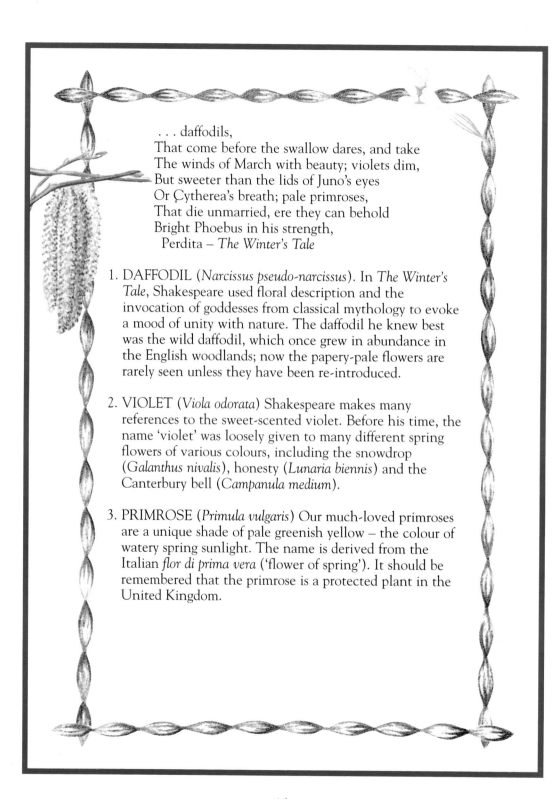

> . . . daffodils,
> That come before the swallow dares, and take
> The winds of March with beauty; violets dim,
> But sweeter than the lids of Juno's eyes
> Or Cytherea's breath; pale primroses,
> That die unmarried, ere they can behold
> Bright Phoebus in his strength,
>   Perdita – *The Winter's Tale*

1. DAFFODIL (*Narcissus pseudo-narcissus*). In *The Winter's Tale*, Shakespeare used floral description and the invocation of goddesses from classical mythology to evoke a mood of unity with nature. The daffodil he knew best was the wild daffodil, which once grew in abundance in the English woodlands; now the papery-pale flowers are rarely seen unless they have been re-introduced.

2. VIOLET (*Viola odorata*) Shakespeare makes many references to the sweet-scented violet. Before his time, the name 'violet' was loosely given to many different spring flowers of various colours, including the snowdrop (*Galanthus nivalis*), honesty (*Lunaria biennis*) and the Canterbury bell (*Campanula medium*).

3. PRIMROSE (*Primula vulgaris*) Our much-loved primroses are a unique shade of pale greenish yellow – the colour of watery spring sunlight. The name is derived from the Italian *flor di prima vera* ('flower of spring'). It should be remembered that the primrose is a protected plant in the United Kingdom.

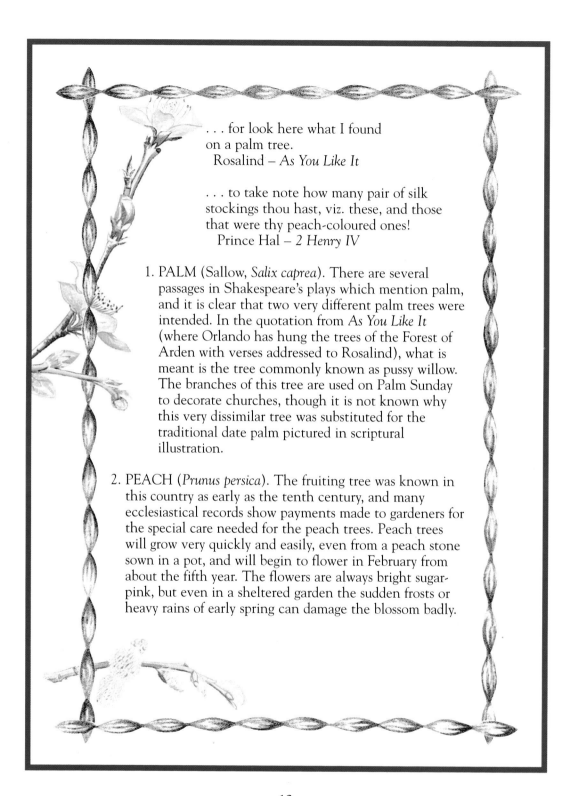

. . . for look here what I found
on a palm tree.
    Rosalind – *As You Like It*

. . . to take note how many pair of silk
stockings thou hast, viz. these, and those
that were thy peach-coloured ones!
    Prince Hal – *2 Henry IV*

1. PALM (Sallow, *Salix caprea*). There are several
passages in Shakespeare's plays which mention palm,
and it is clear that two very different palm trees were
intended. In the quotation from *As You Like It*
(where Orlando has hung the trees of the Forest of
Arden with verses addressed to Rosalind), what is
meant is the tree commonly known as pussy willow.
The branches of this tree are used on Palm Sunday
to decorate churches, though it is not known why
this very dissimilar tree was substituted for the
traditional date palm pictured in scriptural
illustration.

2. PEACH (*Prunus persica*). The fruiting tree was known in
this country as early as the tenth century, and many
ecclesiastical records show payments made to gardeners for
the special care needed for the peach trees. Peach trees
will grow very quickly and easily, even from a peach stone
sown in a pot, and will begin to flower in February from
about the fifth year. The flowers are always bright sugar-
pink, but even in a sheltered garden the sudden frosts or
heavy rains of early spring can damage the blossom badly.

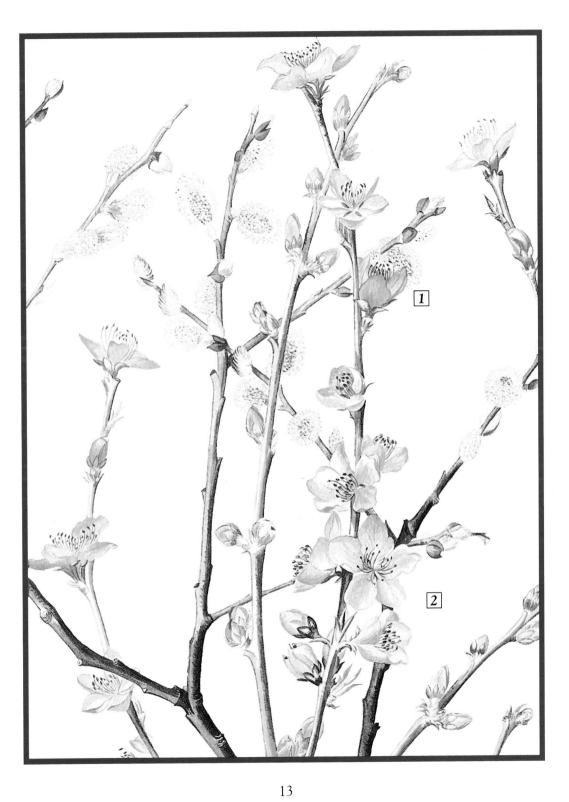

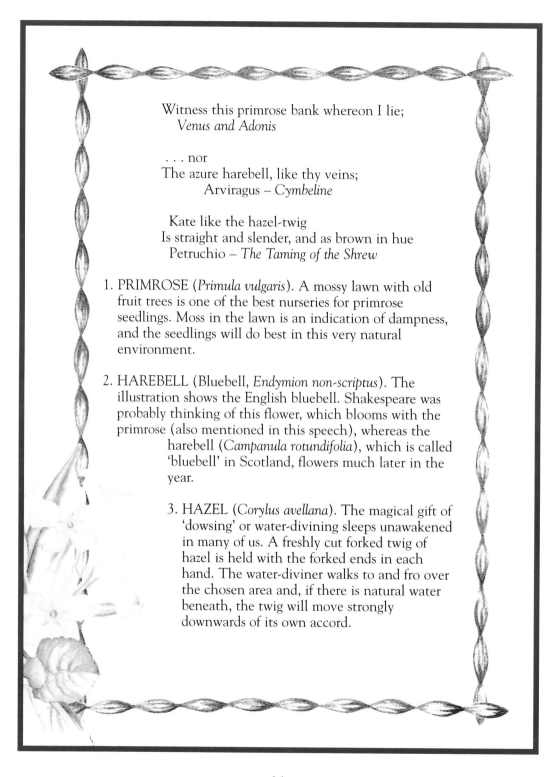

Witness this primrose bank whereon I lie;
Venus and Adonis

. . . nor
The azure harebell, like thy veins;
Arviragus – *Cymbeline*

Kate like the hazel-twig
Is straight and slender, and as brown in hue
Petruchio – *The Taming of the Shrew*

1. PRIMROSE (*Primula vulgaris*). A mossy lawn with old
   fruit trees is one of the best nurseries for primrose
   seedlings. Moss in the lawn is an indication of dampness,
   and the seedlings will do best in this very natural
   environment.

2. HAREBELL (Bluebell, *Endymion non-scriptus*). The
   illustration shows the English bluebell. Shakespeare was
   probably thinking of this flower, which blooms with the
   primrose (also mentioned in this speech), whereas the
   harebell (*Campanula rotundifolia*), which is called
   'bluebell' in Scotland, flowers much later in the
   year.

3. HAZEL (*Corylus avellana*). The magical gift of
   'dowsing' or water-divining sleeps unawakened
   in many of us. A freshly cut forked twig of
   hazel is held with the forked ends in each
   hand. The water-diviner walks to and fro over
   the chosen area and, if there is natural water
   beneath, the twig will move strongly
   downwards of its own accord.

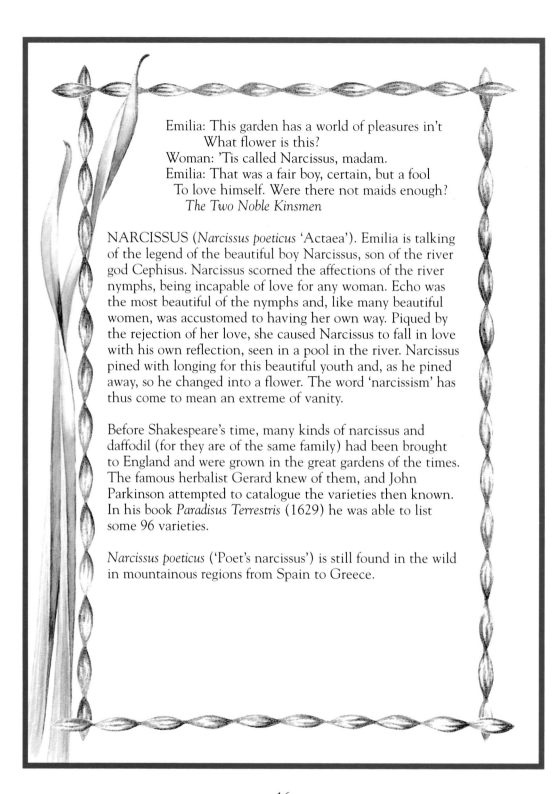

Emilia: This garden has a world of pleasures in't
      What flower is this?
Woman: 'Tis called Narcissus, madam.
Emilia: That was a fair boy, certain, but a fool
    To love himself. Were there not maids enough?
     The Two Noble Kinsmen

NARCISSUS (*Narcissus poeticus* 'Actaea'). Emilia is talking
of the legend of the beautiful boy Narcissus, son of the river
god Cephisus. Narcissus scorned the affections of the river
nymphs, being incapable of love for any woman. Echo was
the most beautiful of the nymphs and, like many beautiful
women, was accustomed to having her own way. Piqued by
the rejection of her love, she caused Narcissus to fall in love
with his own reflection, seen in a pool in the river. Narcissus
pined with longing for this beautiful youth and, as he pined
away, so he changed into a flower. The word 'narcissism' has
thus come to mean an extreme of vanity.

Before Shakespeare's time, many kinds of narcissus and
daffodil (for they are of the same family) had been brought
to England and were grown in the great gardens of the times.
The famous herbalist Gerard knew of them, and John
Parkinson attempted to catalogue the varieties then known.
In his book *Paradisus Terrestris* (1629) he was able to list
some 96 varieties.

Narcissus poeticus ('Poet's narcissus') is still found in the wild
in mountainous regions from Spain to Greece.

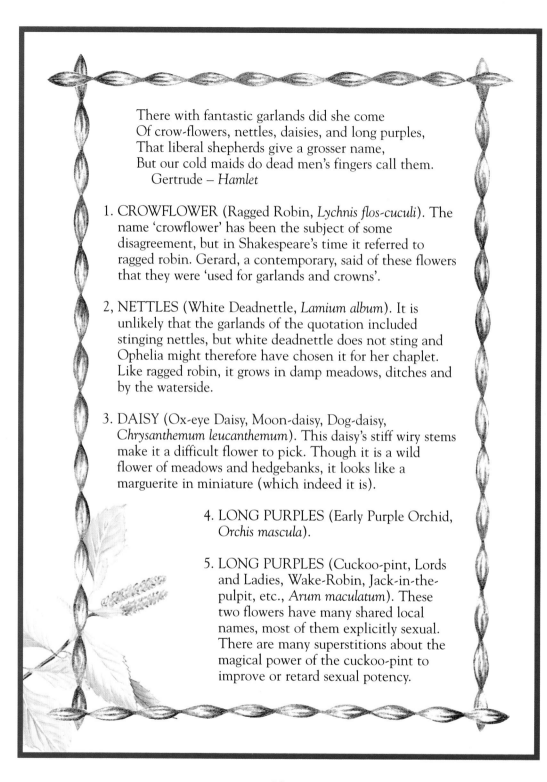

There with fantastic garlands did she come
Of crow-flowers, nettles, daisies, and long purples,
That liberal shepherds give a grosser name,
But our cold maids do dead men's fingers call them.
    Gertrude – *Hamlet*

1. CROWFLOWER (Ragged Robin, *Lychnis flos-cuculi*). The name 'crowflower' has been the subject of some disagreement, but in Shakespeare's time it referred to ragged robin. Gerard, a contemporary, said of these flowers that they were 'used for garlands and crowns'.

2, NETTLES (White Deadnettle, *Lamium album*). It is unlikely that the garlands of the quotation included stinging nettles, but white deadnettle does not sting and Ophelia might therefore have chosen it for her chaplet. Like ragged robin, it grows in damp meadows, ditches and by the waterside.

3. DAISY (Ox-eye Daisy, Moon-daisy, Dog-daisy, *Chrysanthemum leucanthemum*). This daisy's stiff wiry stems make it a difficult flower to pick. Though it is a wild flower of meadows and hedgebanks, it looks like a marguerite in miniature (which indeed it is).

4. LONG PURPLES (Early Purple Orchid, *Orchis mascula*).

5. LONG PURPLES (Cuckoo-pint, Lords and Ladies, Wake-Robin, Jack-in-the-pulpit, etc., *Arum maculatum*). These two flowers have many shared local names, most of them explicitly sexual. There are many superstitions about the magical power of the cuckoo-pint to improve or retard sexual potency.

19

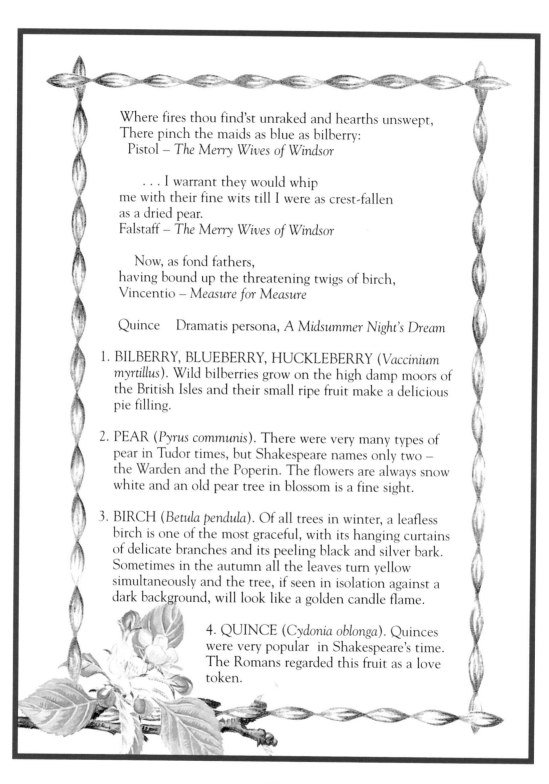

Where fires thou find'st unraked and hearths unswept,
There pinch the maids as blue as bilberry:
  Pistol – *The Merry Wives of Windsor*

    . . . I warrant they would whip
me with their fine wits till I were as crest-fallen
as a dried pear.
Falstaff – *The Merry Wives of Windsor*

   Now, as fond fathers,
having bound up the threatening twigs of birch,
Vincentio – *Measure for Measure*

Quince   Dramatis persona, *A Midsummer Night's Dream*

1. BILBERRY, BLUEBERRY, HUCKLEBERRY (*Vaccinium myrtillus*). Wild bilberries grow on the high damp moors of the British Isles and their small ripe fruit make a delicious pie filling.

2. PEAR (*Pyrus communis*). There were very many types of pear in Tudor times, but Shakespeare names only two – the Warden and the Poperin. The flowers are always snow white and an old pear tree in blossom is a fine sight.

3. BIRCH (*Betula pendula*). Of all trees in winter, a leafless birch is one of the most graceful, with its hanging curtains of delicate branches and its peeling black and silver bark. Sometimes in the autumn all the leaves turn yellow simultaneously and the tree, if seen in isolation against a dark background, will look like a golden candle flame.

4. QUINCE (*Cydonia oblonga*). Quinces were very popular in Shakespeare's time. The Romans regarded this fruit as a love token.

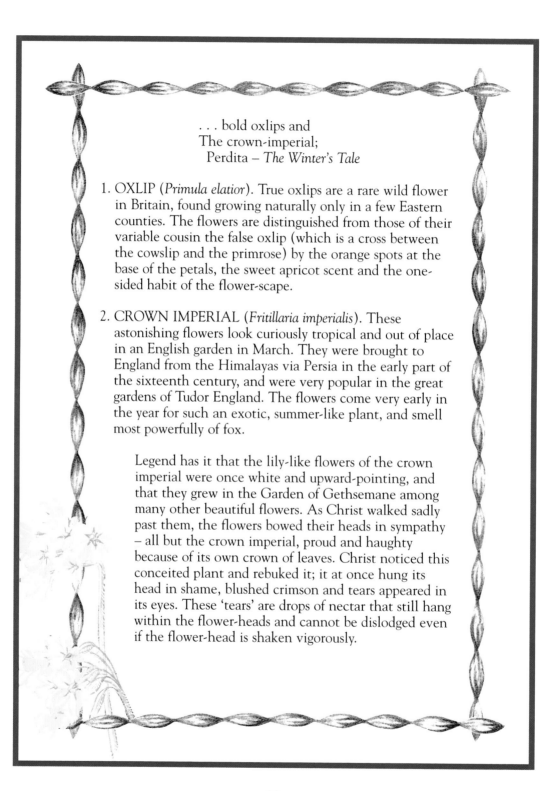

> . . . bold oxlips and
> The crown-imperial;
> Perdita – *The Winter's Tale*

1. OXLIP (*Primula elatior*). True oxlips are a rare wild flower
   in Britain, found growing naturally only in a few Eastern
   counties. The flowers are distinguished from those of their
   variable cousin the false oxlip (which is a cross between
   the cowslip and the primrose) by the orange spots at the
   base of the petals, the sweet apricot scent and the one-
   sided habit of the flower-scape.

2. CROWN IMPERIAL (*Fritillaria imperialis*). These
   astonishing flowers look curiously tropical and out of place
   in an English garden in March. They were brought to
   England from the Himalayas via Persia in the early part of
   the sixteenth century, and were very popular in the great
   gardens of Tudor England. The flowers come very early in
   the year for such an exotic, summer-like plant, and smell
   most powerfully of fox.

   > Legend has it that the lily-like flowers of the crown
   > imperial were once white and upward-pointing, and
   > that they grew in the Garden of Gethsemane among
   > many other beautiful flowers. As Christ walked sadly
   > past them, the flowers bowed their heads in sympathy
   > – all but the crown imperial, proud and haughty
   > because of its own crown of leaves. Christ noticed this
   > conceited plant and rebuked it; it at once hung its
   > head in shame, blushed crimson and tears appeared in
   > its eyes. These 'tears' are drops of nectar that still hang
   > within the flower-heads and cannot be dislodged even
   > if the flower-head is shaken vigorously.

2

1

23

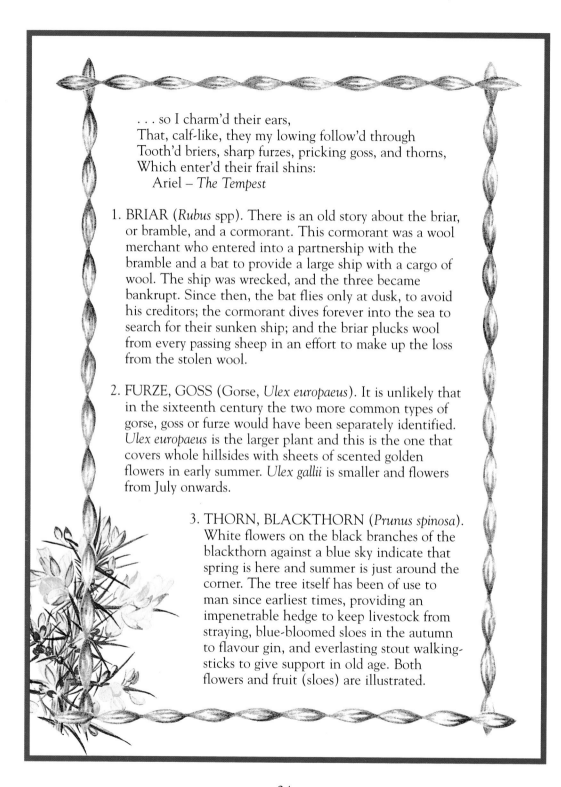

    . . . so I charm'd their ears,
That, calf-like, they my lowing follow'd through
Tooth'd briers, sharp furzes, pricking goss, and thorns,
Which enter'd their frail shins:
    Ariel – *The Tempest*

1. BRIAR (*Rubus* spp). There is an old story about the briar, or bramble, and a cormorant. This cormorant was a wool merchant who entered into a partnership with the bramble and a bat to provide a large ship with a cargo of wool. The ship was wrecked, and the three became bankrupt. Since then, the bat flies only at dusk, to avoid his creditors; the cormorant dives forever into the sea to search for their sunken ship; and the briar plucks wool from every passing sheep in an effort to make up the loss from the stolen wool.

2. FURZE, GOSS (Gorse, *Ulex europaeus*). It is unlikely that in the sixteenth century the two more common types of gorse, goss or furze would have been separately identified. *Ulex europaeus* is the larger plant and this is the one that covers whole hillsides with sheets of scented golden flowers in early summer. *Ulex gallii* is smaller and flowers from July onwards.

3. THORN, BLACKTHORN (*Prunus spinosa*). White flowers on the black branches of the blackthorn against a blue sky indicate that spring is here and summer is just around the corner. The tree itself has been of use to man since earliest times, providing an impenetrable hedge to keep livestock from straying, blue-bloomed sloes in the autumn to flavour gin, and everlasting stout walking-sticks to give support in old age. Both flowers and fruit (sloes) are illustrated.

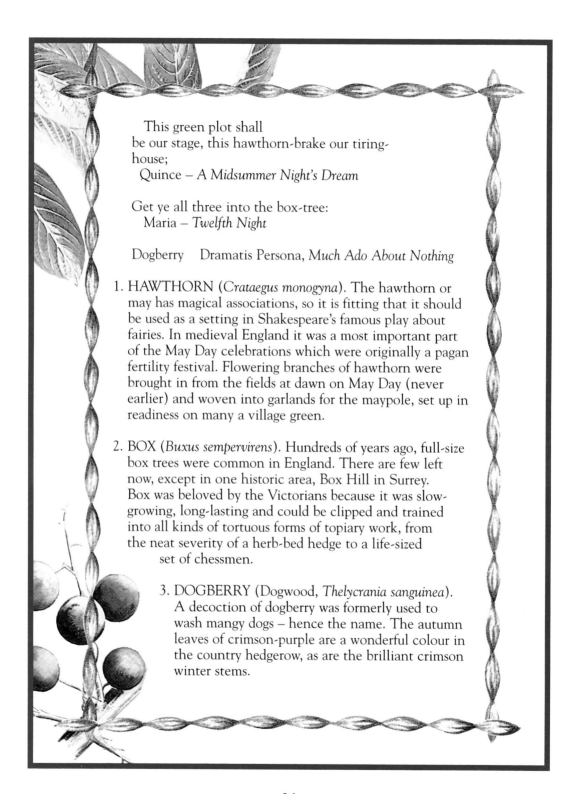

This green plot shall
be our stage, this hawthorn-brake our tiring-
house;
   Quince – *A Midsummer Night's Dream*

Get ye all three into the box-tree:
   Maria – *Twelfth Night*

Dogberry   Dramatis Persona, *Much Ado About Nothing*

1. HAWTHORN (*Crataegus monogyna*). The hawthorn or may has magical associations, so it is fitting that it should be used as a setting in Shakespeare's famous play about fairies. In medieval England it was a most important part of the May Day celebrations which were originally a pagan fertility festival. Flowering branches of hawthorn were brought in from the fields at dawn on May Day (never earlier) and woven into garlands for the maypole, set up in readiness on many a village green.

2. BOX (*Buxus sempervirens*). Hundreds of years ago, full-size box trees were common in England. There are few left now, except in one historic area, Box Hill in Surrey. Box was beloved by the Victorians because it was slow-growing, long-lasting and could be clipped and trained into all kinds of tortuous forms of topiary work, from the neat severity of a herb-bed hedge to a life-sized set of chessmen.

3. DOGBERRY (Dogwood, *Thelycrania sanguinea*). A decoction of dogberry was formerly used to wash mangy dogs – hence the name. The autumn leaves of crimson-purple are a wonderful colour in the country hedgerow, as are the brilliant crimson winter stems.

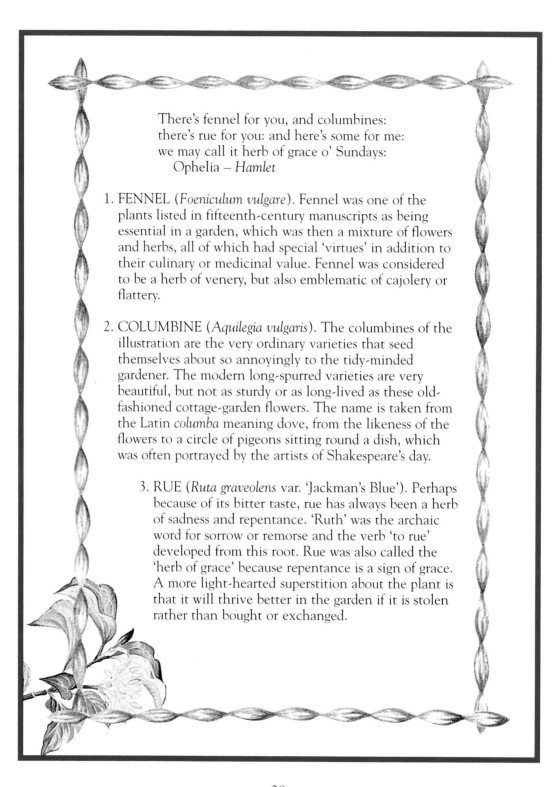

There's fennel for you, and columbines:
there's rue for you: and here's some for me:
we may call it herb of grace o' Sundays:
Ophelia – *Hamlet*

1. FENNEL (*Foeniculum vulgare*). Fennel was one of the plants listed in fifteenth-century manuscripts as being essential in a garden, which was then a mixture of flowers and herbs, all of which had special 'virtues' in addition to their culinary or medicinal value. Fennel was considered to be a herb of venery, but also emblematic of cajolery or flattery.

2. COLUMBINE (*Aquilegia vulgaris*). The columbines of the illustration are the very ordinary varieties that seed themselves about so annoyingly to the tidy-minded gardener. The modern long-spurred varieties are very beautiful, but not as sturdy or as long-lived as these old-fashioned cottage-garden flowers. The name is taken from the Latin *columba* meaning dove, from the likeness of the flowers to a circle of pigeons sitting round a dish, which was often portrayed by the artists of Shakespeare's day.

3. RUE (*Ruta graveolens* var. 'Jackman's Blue'). Perhaps because of its bitter taste, rue has always been a herb of sadness and repentance. 'Ruth' was the archaic word for sorrow or remorse and the verb 'to rue' developed from this root. Rue was also called the 'herb of grace' because repentance is a sign of grace. A more light-hearted superstition about the plant is that it will thrive better in the garden if it is stolen rather than bought or exchanged.

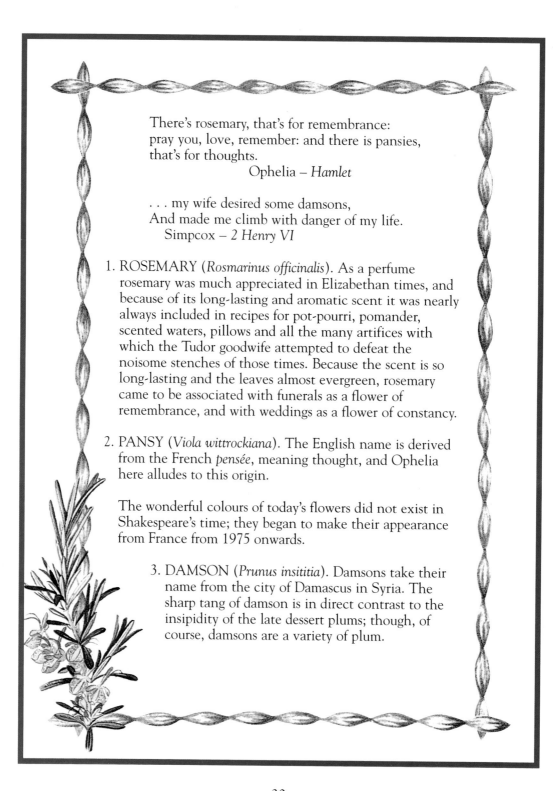

There's rosemary, that's for remembrance:
pray you, love, remember: and there is pansies,
that's for thoughts.
                    Ophelia – *Hamlet*

. . . my wife desired some damsons,
And made me climb with danger of my life.
            Simpcox – *2 Henry VI*

1. ROSEMARY (*Rosmarinus officinalis*). As a perfume
   rosemary was much appreciated in Elizabethan times, and
   because of its long-lasting and aromatic scent it was nearly
   always included in recipes for pot-pourri, pomander,
   scented waters, pillows and all the many artifices with
   which the Tudor goodwife attempted to defeat the
   noisome stenches of those times. Because the scent is so
   long-lasting and the leaves almost evergreen, rosemary
   came to be associated with funerals as a flower of
   remembrance, and with weddings as a flower of constancy.

2. PANSY (*Viola wittrockiana*). The English name is derived
   from the French *pensée*, meaning thought, and Ophelia
   here alludes to this origin.

   The wonderful colours of today's flowers did not exist in
   Shakespeare's time; they began to make their appearance
   from France from 1975 onwards.

3. DAMSON (*Prunus insititia*). Damsons take their
   name from the city of Damascus in Syria. The
   sharp tang of damson is in direct contrast to the
   insipidity of the late dessert plums; though, of
   course, damsons are a variety of plum.

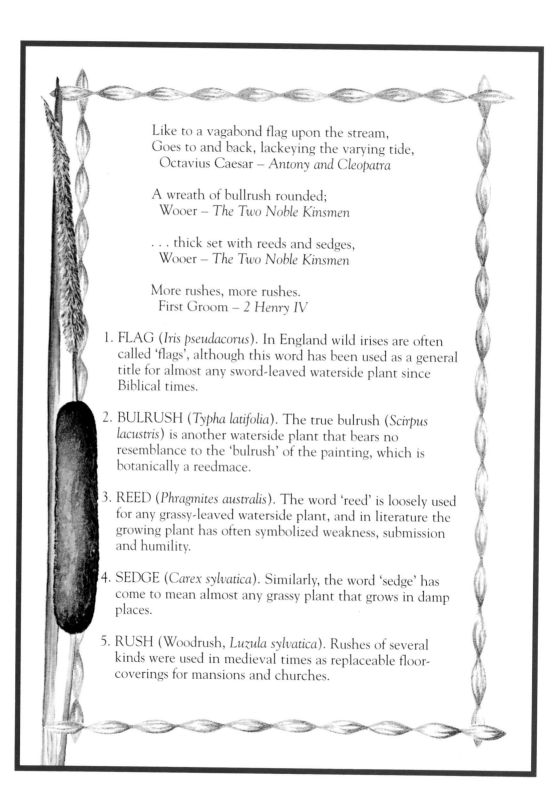

Like to a vagabond flag upon the stream,
Goes to and back, lackeying the varying tide,
  Octavius Caesar – *Antony and Cleopatra*

A wreath of bullrush rounded;
  Wooer – *The Two Noble Kinsmen*

. . . thick set with reeds and sedges,
  Wooer – *The Two Noble Kinsmen*

More rushes, more rushes.
  First Groom – *2 Henry IV*

1. FLAG (*Iris pseudacorus*). In England wild irises are often
   called 'flags', although this word has been used as a general
   title for almost any sword-leaved waterside plant since
   Biblical times.

2. BULRUSH (*Typha latifolia*). The true bulrush (*Scirpus
   lacustris*) is another waterside plant that bears no
   resemblance to the 'bulrush' of the painting, which is
   botanically a reedmace.

3. REED (*Phragmites australis*). The word 'reed' is loosely used
   for any grassy-leaved waterside plant, and in literature the
   growing plant has often symbolized weakness, submission
   and humility.

4. SEDGE (*Carex sylvatica*). Similarly, the word 'sedge' has
   come to mean almost any grassy plant that grows in damp
   places.

5. RUSH (Woodrush, *Luzula sylvatica*). Rushes of several
   kinds were used in medieval times as replaceable floor-
   coverings for mansions and churches.

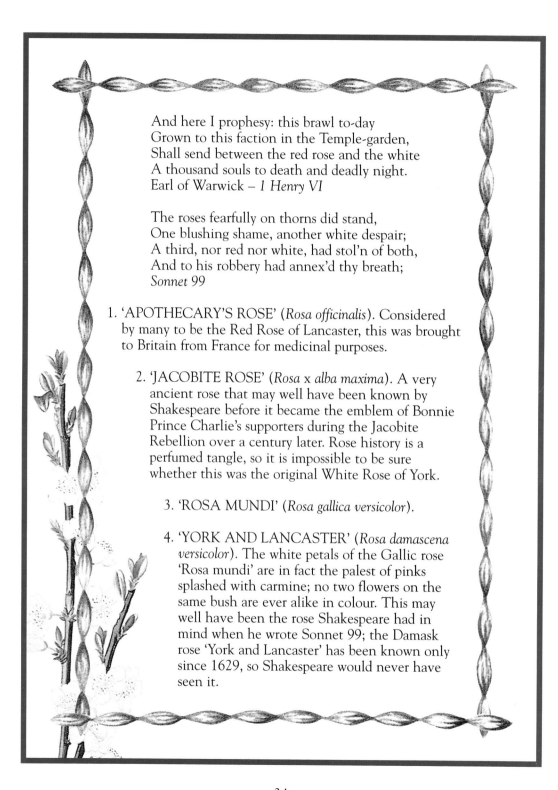

And here I prophesy: this brawl to-day
Grown to this faction in the Temple-garden,
Shall send between the red rose and the white
A thousand souls to death and deadly night.
Earl of Warwick – *1 Henry VI*

The roses fearfully on thorns did stand,
One blushing shame, another white despair;
A third, nor red nor white, had stol'n of both,
And to his robbery had annex'd thy breath;
Sonnet 99

1. 'APOTHECARY'S ROSE' (*Rosa officinalis*). Considered by many to be the Red Rose of Lancaster, this was brought to Britain from France for medicinal purposes.

2. 'JACOBITE ROSE' (*Rosa* x *alba maxima*). A very ancient rose that may well have been known by Shakespeare before it became the emblem of Bonnie Prince Charlie's supporters during the Jacobite Rebellion over a century later. Rose history is a perfumed tangle, so it is impossible to be sure whether this was the original White Rose of York.

3. 'ROSA MUNDI' (*Rosa gallica versicolor*).

4. 'YORK AND LANCASTER' (*Rosa damascena versicolor*). The white petals of the Gallic rose 'Rosa mundi' are in fact the palest of pinks splashed with carmine; no two flowers on the same bush are ever alike in colour. This may well have been the rose Shakespeare had in mind when he wrote Sonnet 99; the Damask rose 'York and Lancaster' has been known only since 1629, so Shakespeare would never have seen it.

35

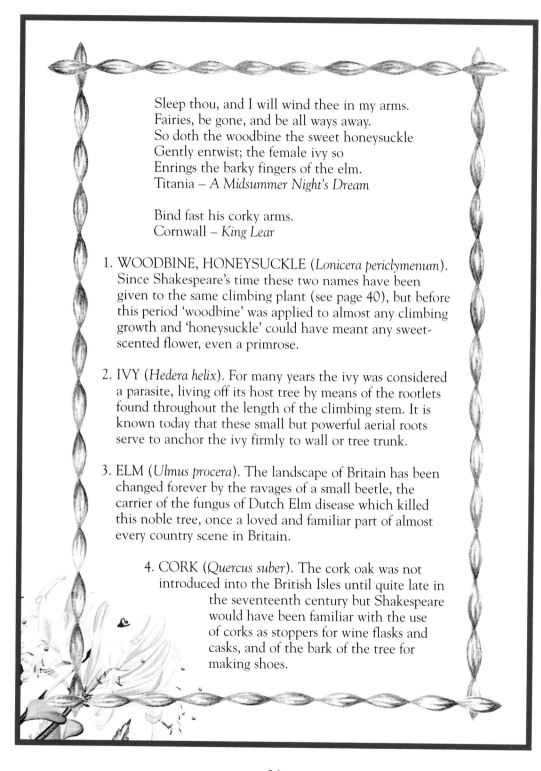

Sleep thou, and I will wind thee in my arms.
Fairies, be gone, and be all ways away.
So doth the woodbine the sweet honeysuckle
Gently entwist; the female ivy so
Enrings the barky fingers of the elm.
Titania – *A Midsummer Night's Dream*

Bind fast his corky arms.
Cornwall – *King Lear*

1. WOODBINE, HONEYSUCKLE (*Lonicera periclymenum*).
   Since Shakespeare's time these two names have been
   given to the same climbing plant (see page 40), but before
   this period 'woodbine' was applied to almost any climbing
   growth and 'honeysuckle' could have meant any sweet-
   scented flower, even a primrose.

2. IVY (*Hedera helix*). For many years the ivy was considered
   a parasite, living off its host tree by means of the rootlets
   found throughout the length of the climbing stem. It is
   known today that these small but powerful aerial roots
   serve to anchor the ivy firmly to wall or tree trunk.

3. ELM (*Ulmus procera*). The landscape of Britain has been
   changed forever by the ravages of a small beetle, the
   carrier of the fungus of Dutch Elm disease which killed
   this noble tree, once a loved and familiar part of almost
   every country scene in Britain.

4. CORK (*Quercus suber*). The cork oak was not
   introduced into the British Isles until quite late in
   the seventeenth century but Shakespeare
   would have been familiar with the use
   of corks as stoppers for wine flasks and
   casks, and of the bark of the tree for
   making shoes.

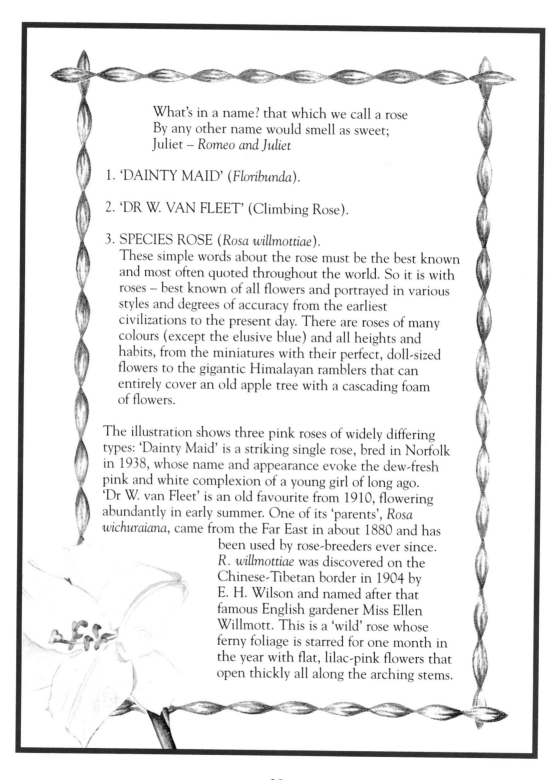

What's in a name? that which we call a rose
By any other name would smell as sweet;
Juliet – *Romeo and Juliet*

1. 'DAINTY MAID' (*Floribunda*).

2. 'DR W. VAN FLEET' (Climbing Rose).

3. SPECIES ROSE (*Rosa willmottiae*).
   These simple words about the rose must be the best known
   and most often quoted throughout the world. So it is with
   roses – best known of all flowers and portrayed in various
   styles and degrees of accuracy from the earliest
   civilizations to the present day. There are roses of many
   colours (except the elusive blue) and all heights and
   habits, from the miniatures with their perfect, doll-sized
   flowers to the gigantic Himalayan ramblers that can
   entirely cover an old apple tree with a cascading foam
   of flowers.

The illustration shows three pink roses of widely differing
types: 'Dainty Maid' is a striking single rose, bred in Norfolk
in 1938, whose name and appearance evoke the dew-fresh
pink and white complexion of a young girl of long ago.
'Dr W. van Fleet' is an old favourite from 1910, flowering
abundantly in early summer. One of its 'parents', *Rosa
wichuraiana*, came from the Far East in about 1880 and has
been used by rose-breeders ever since.
R. willmottiae was discovered on the
Chinese-Tibetan border in 1904 by
E. H. Wilson and named after that
famous English gardener Miss Ellen
Willmott. This is a 'wild' rose whose
ferny foliage is starred for one month in
the year with flat, lilac-pink flowers that
open thickly all along the arching stems.

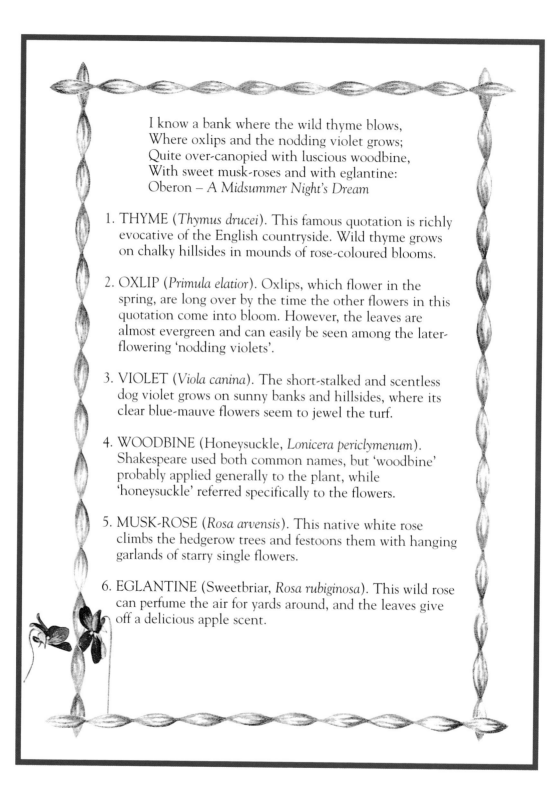

I know a bank where the wild thyme blows,
Where oxlips and the nodding violet grows;
Quite over-canopied with luscious woodbine,
With sweet musk-roses and with eglantine:
Oberon – A *Midsummer Night's Dream*

1. THYME (*Thymus drucei*). This famous quotation is richly
   evocative of the English countryside. Wild thyme grows
   on chalky hillsides in mounds of rose-coloured blooms.

2. OXLIP (*Primula elatior*). Oxlips, which flower in the
   spring, are long over by the time the other flowers in this
   quotation come into bloom. However, the leaves are
   almost evergreen and can easily be seen among the later-
   flowering 'nodding violets'.

3. VIOLET (*Viola canina*). The short-stalked and scentless
   dog violet grows on sunny banks and hillsides, where its
   clear blue-mauve flowers seem to jewel the turf.

4. WOODBINE (Honeysuckle, *Lonicera periclymenum*).
   Shakespeare used both common names, but 'woodbine'
   probably applied generally to the plant, while
   'honeysuckle' referred specifically to the flowers.

5. MUSK-ROSE (*Rosa arvensis*). This native white rose
   climbs the hedgerow trees and festoons them with hanging
   garlands of starry single flowers.

6. EGLANTINE (Sweetbriar, *Rosa rubiginosa*). This wild rose
   can perfume the air for yards around, and the leaves give
   off a delicious apple scent.

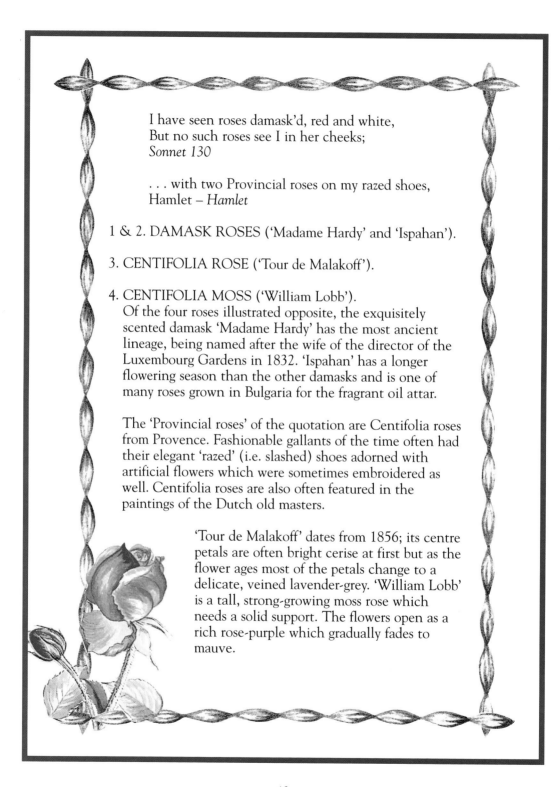

I have seen roses damask'd, red and white,
But no such roses see I in her cheeks;
Sonnet 130

. . . with two Provincial roses on my razed shoes,
Hamlet – *Hamlet*

1 & 2. DAMASK ROSES ('Madame Hardy' and 'Ispahan').

3. CENTIFOLIA ROSE ('Tour de Malakoff').

4. CENTIFOLIA MOSS ('William Lobb').
Of the four roses illustrated opposite, the exquisitely
scented damask 'Madame Hardy' has the most ancient
lineage, being named after the wife of the director of the
Luxembourg Gardens in 1832. 'Ispahan' has a longer
flowering season than the other damasks and is one of
many roses grown in Bulgaria for the fragrant oil attar.

The 'Provincial roses' of the quotation are Centifolia roses
from Provence. Fashionable gallants of the time often had
their elegant 'razed' (i.e. slashed) shoes adorned with
artificial flowers which were sometimes embroidered as
well. Centifolia roses are also often featured in the
paintings of the Dutch old masters.

'Tour de Malakoff' dates from 1856; its centre
petals are often bright cerise at first but as the
flower ages most of the petals change to a
delicate, veined lavender-grey. 'William Lobb'
is a tall, strong-growing moss rose which
needs a solid support. The flowers open as a
rich rose-purple which gradually fades to
mauve.

43

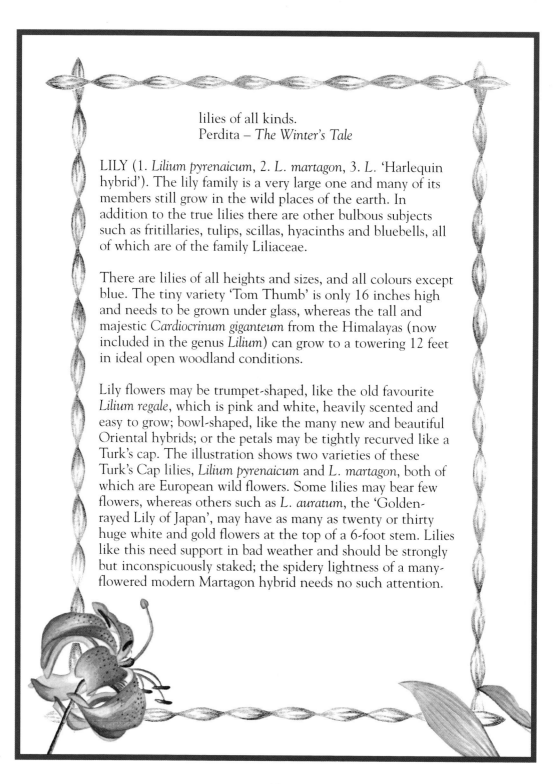

lilies of all kinds.
Perdita – *The Winter's Tale*

LILY (1. *Lilium pyrenaicum*, 2. *L. martagon*, 3. *L.* 'Harlequin hybrid'). The lily family is a very large one and many of its members still grow in the wild places of the earth. In addition to the true lilies there are other bulbous subjects such as fritillaries, tulips, scillas, hyacinths and bluebells, all of which are of the family Liliaceae.

There are lilies of all heights and sizes, and all colours except blue. The tiny variety 'Tom Thumb' is only 16 inches high and needs to be grown under glass, whereas the tall and majestic *Cardiocrinum giganteum* from the Himalayas (now included in the genus *Lilium*) can grow to a towering 12 feet in ideal open woodland conditions.

Lily flowers may be trumpet-shaped, like the old favourite *Lilium regale*, which is pink and white, heavily scented and easy to grow; bowl-shaped, like the many new and beautiful Oriental hybrids; or the petals may be tightly recurved like a Turk's cap. The illustration shows two varieties of these Turk's Cap lilies, *Lilium pyrenaicum* and *L. martagon*, both of which are European wild flowers. Some lilies may bear few flowers, whereas others such as *L. auratum*, the 'Golden-rayed Lily of Japan', may have as many as twenty or thirty huge white and gold flowers at the top of a 6-foot stem. Lilies like this need support in bad weather and should be strongly but inconspicuously staked; the spidery lightness of a many-flowered modern Martagon hybrid needs no such attention.

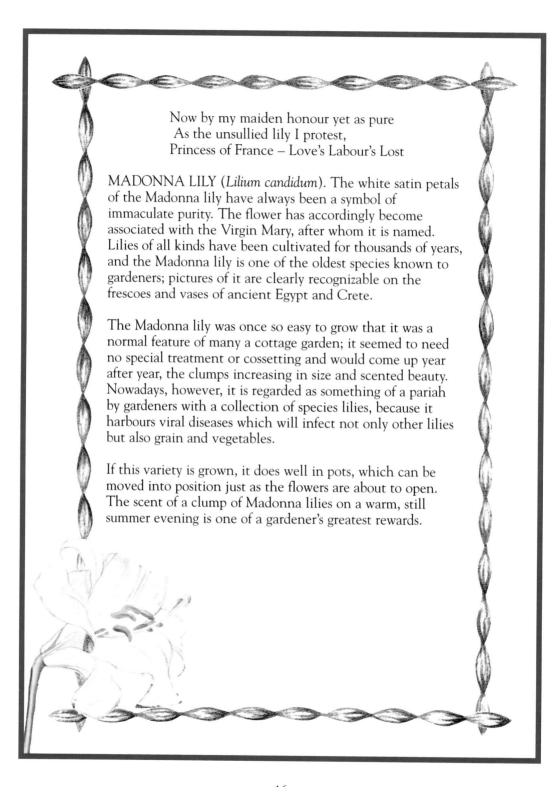

Now by my maiden honour yet as pure
As the unsullied lily I protest,
Princess of France – Love's Labour's Lost

MADONNA LILY (*Lilium candidum*). The white satin petals of the Madonna lily have always been a symbol of immaculate purity. The flower has accordingly become associated with the Virgin Mary, after whom it is named. Lilies of all kinds have been cultivated for thousands of years, and the Madonna lily is one of the oldest species known to gardeners; pictures of it are clearly recognizable on the frescoes and vases of ancient Egypt and Crete.

The Madonna lily was once so easy to grow that it was a normal feature of many a cottage garden; it seemed to need no special treatment or cossetting and would come up year after year, the clumps increasing in size and scented beauty. Nowadays, however, it is regarded as something of a pariah by gardeners with a collection of species lilies, because it harbours viral diseases which will infect not only other lilies but also grain and vegetables.

If this variety is grown, it does well in pots, which can be moved into position just as the flowers are about to open. The scent of a clump of Madonna lilies on a warm, still summer evening is one of a gardener's greatest rewards.

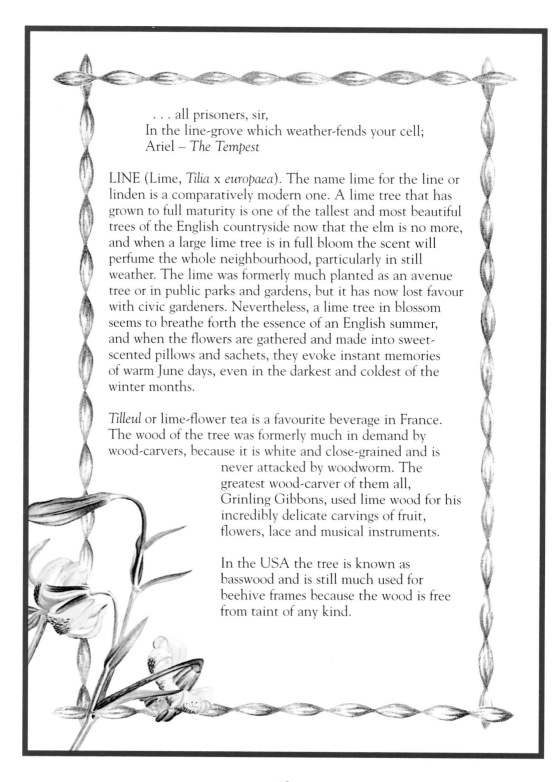

. . . all prisoners, sir,
In the line-grove which weather-fends your cell;
Ariel – *The Tempest*

LINE (Lime, *Tilia* x *europaea*). The name lime for the line or linden is a comparatively modern one. A lime tree that has grown to full maturity is one of the tallest and most beautiful trees of the English countryside now that the elm is no more, and when a large lime tree is in full bloom the scent will perfume the whole neighbourhood, particularly in still weather. The lime was formerly much planted as an avenue tree or in public parks and gardens, but it has now lost favour with civic gardeners. Nevertheless, a lime tree in blossom seems to breathe forth the essence of an English summer, and when the flowers are gathered and made into sweet-scented pillows and sachets, they evoke instant memories of warm June days, even in the darkest and coldest of the winter months.

Tilleul or lime-flower tea is a favourite beverage in France. The wood of the tree was formerly much in demand by wood-carvers, because it is white and close-grained and is never attacked by woodworm. The greatest wood-carver of them all, Grinling Gibbons, used lime wood for his incredibly delicate carvings of fruit, flowers, lace and musical instruments.

In the USA the tree is known as basswood and is still much used for beehive frames because the wood is free from taint of any kind.

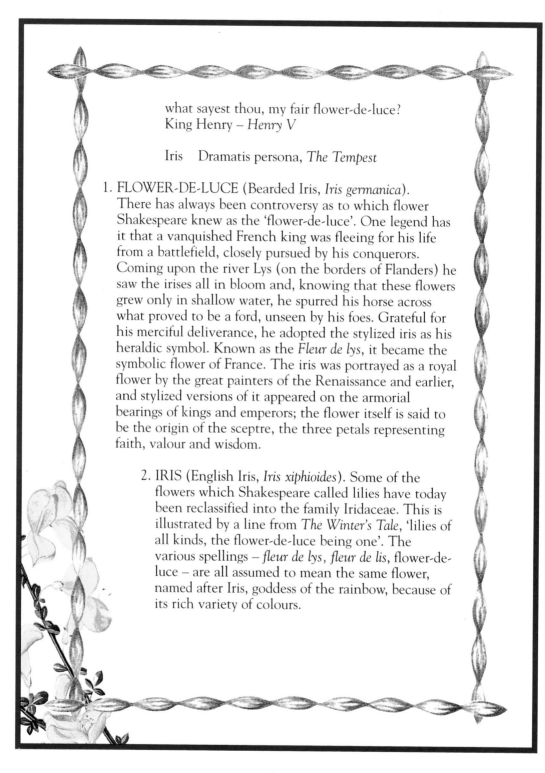

what sayest thou, my fair flower-de-luce?
King Henry – *Henry V*

Iris   Dramatis persona, *The Tempest*

1. FLOWER-DE-LUCE (Bearded Iris, *Iris germanica*).
There has always been controversy as to which flower
Shakespeare knew as the 'flower-de-luce'. One legend has
it that a vanquished French king was fleeing for his life
from a battlefield, closely pursued by his conquerors.
Coming upon the river Lys (on the borders of Flanders) he
saw the irises all in bloom and, knowing that these flowers
grew only in shallow water, he spurred his horse across
what proved to be a ford, unseen by his foes. Grateful for
his merciful deliverance, he adopted the stylized iris as his
heraldic symbol. Known as the *Fleur de lys*, it became the
symbolic flower of France. The iris was portrayed as a royal
flower by the great painters of the Renaissance and earlier,
and stylized versions of it appeared on the armorial
bearings of kings and emperors; the flower itself is said to
be the origin of the sceptre, the three petals representing
faith, valour and wisdom.

2. IRIS (English Iris, *Iris xiphioides*). Some of the
flowers which Shakespeare called lilies have today
been reclassified into the family Iridaceae. This is
illustrated by a line from *The Winter's Tale*, 'lilies of
all kinds, the flower-de-luce being one'. The
various spellings – *fleur de lys, fleur de lis*, flower-de-
luce – are all assumed to mean the same flower,
named after Iris, goddess of the rainbow, because of
its rich variety of colours.

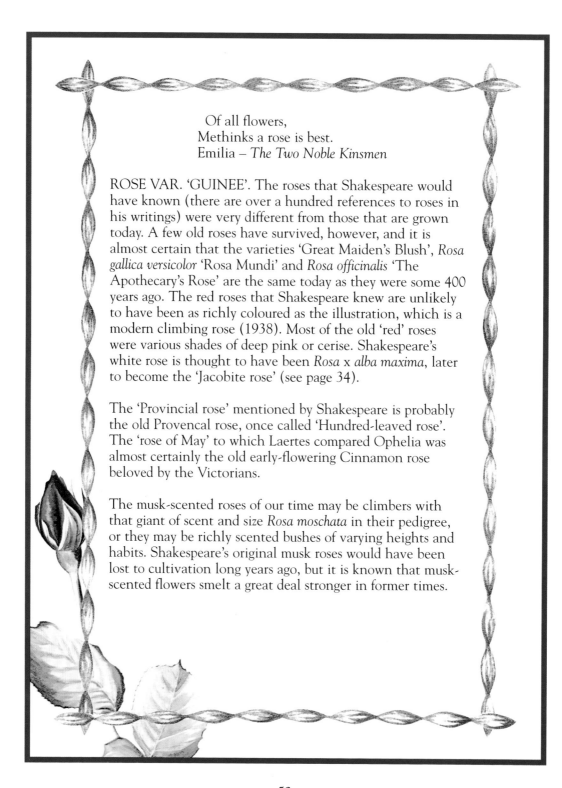

Of all flowers,
Methinks a rose is best.
Emilia – *The Two Noble Kinsmen*

ROSE VAR. 'GUINEE'. The roses that Shakespeare would have known (there are over a hundred references to roses in his writings) were very different from those that are grown today. A few old roses have survived, however, and it is almost certain that the varieties 'Great Maiden's Blush', *Rosa gallica versicolor* 'Rosa Mundi' and *Rosa officinalis* 'The Apothecary's Rose' are the same today as they were some 400 years ago. The red roses that Shakespeare knew are unlikely to have been as richly coloured as the illustration, which is a modern climbing rose (1938). Most of the old 'red' roses were various shades of deep pink or cerise. Shakespeare's white rose is thought to have been *Rosa x alba maxima*, later to become the 'Jacobite rose' (see page 34).

The 'Provincial rose' mentioned by Shakespeare is probably the old Provencal rose, once called 'Hundred-leaved rose'. The 'rose of May' to which Laertes compared Ophelia was almost certainly the old early-flowering Cinnamon rose beloved by the Victorians.

The musk-scented roses of our time may be climbers with that giant of scent and size *Rosa moschata* in their pedigree, or they may be richly scented bushes of varying heights and habits. Shakespeare's original musk roses would have been lost to cultivation long years ago, but it is known that musk-scented flowers smelt a great deal stronger in former times.

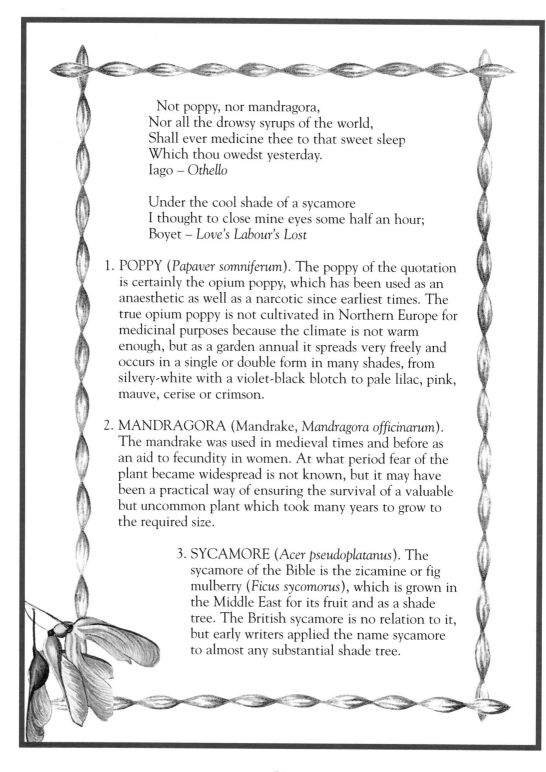

Not poppy, nor mandragora,
Nor all the drowsy syrups of the world,
Shall ever medicine thee to that sweet sleep
Which thou owedst yesterday.
Iago – *Othello*

Under the cool shade of a sycamore
I thought to close mine eyes some half an hour;
Boyet – *Love's Labour's Lost*

1. POPPY (*Papaver somniferum*). The poppy of the quotation is certainly the opium poppy, which has been used as an anaesthetic as well as a narcotic since earliest times. The true opium poppy is not cultivated in Northern Europe for medicinal purposes because the climate is not warm enough, but as a garden annual it spreads very freely and occurs in a single or double form in many shades, from silvery-white with a violet-black blotch to pale lilac, pink, mauve, cerise or crimson.

2. MANDRAGORA (Mandrake, *Mandragora officinarum*). The mandrake was used in medieval times and before as an aid to fecundity in women. At what period fear of the plant became widespread is not known, but it may have been a practical way of ensuring the survival of a valuable but uncommon plant which took many years to grow to the required size.

3. SYCAMORE (*Acer pseudoplatanus*). The sycamore of the Bible is the zicamine or fig mulberry (*Ficus sycomorus*), which is grown in the Middle East for its fruit and as a shade tree. The British sycamore is no relation to it, but early writers applied the name sycamore to almost any substantial shade tree.

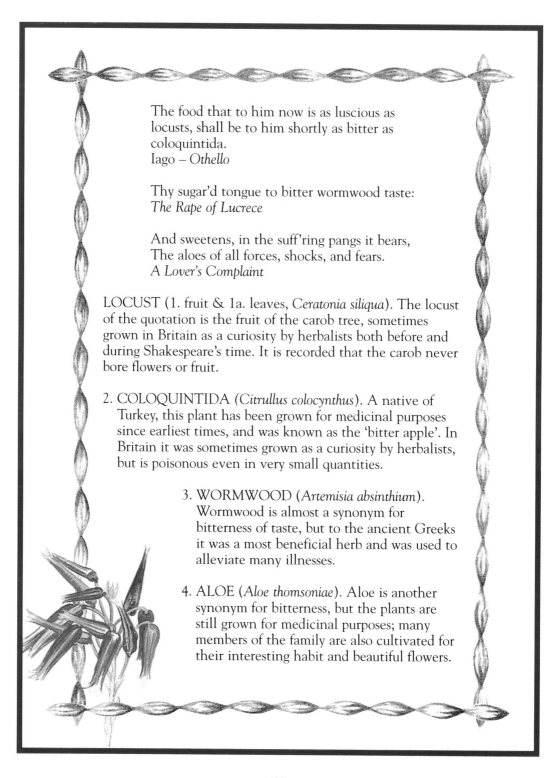

The food that to him now is as luscious as locusts, shall be to him shortly as bitter as coloquintida.
Iago – *Othello*

Thy sugar'd tongue to bitter wormwood taste:
The Rape of Lucrece

And sweetens, in the suff'ring pangs it bears,
The aloes of all forces, shocks, and fears.
A *Lover's Complaint*

LOCUST (1. fruit & 1a. leaves, *Ceratonia siliqua*). The locust of the quotation is the fruit of the carob tree, sometimes grown in Britain as a curiosity by herbalists both before and during Shakespeare's time. It is recorded that the carob never bore flowers or fruit.

2. COLOQUINTIDA (*Citrullus colocynthus*). A native of Turkey, this plant has been grown for medicinal purposes since earliest times, and was known as the 'bitter apple'. In Britain it was sometimes grown as a curiosity by herbalists, but is poisonous even in very small quantities.

3. WORMWOOD (*Artemisia absinthium*). Wormwood is almost a synonym for bitterness of taste, but to the ancient Greeks it was a most beneficial herb and was used to alleviate many illnesses.

4. ALOE (*Aloe thomsoniae*). Aloe is another synonym for bitterness, but the plants are still grown for medicinal purposes; many members of the family are also cultivated for their interesting habit and beautiful flowers.

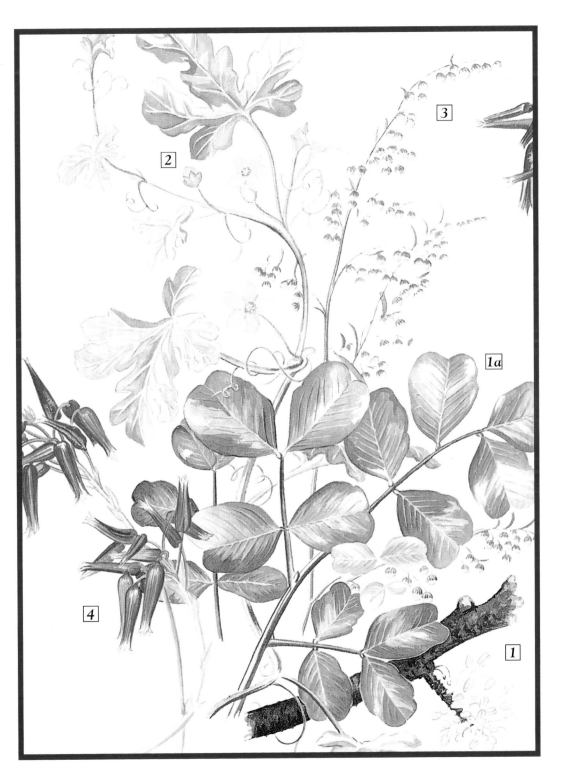

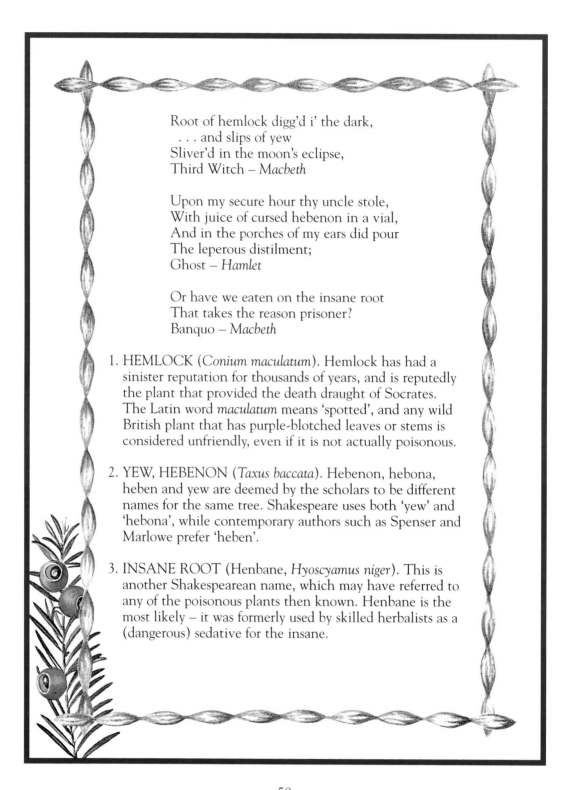

Root of hemlock digg'd i' the dark,
 . . . and slips of yew
Sliver'd in the moon's eclipse,
Third Witch – *Macbeth*

Upon my secure hour thy uncle stole,
With juice of cursed hebenon in a vial,
And in the porches of my ears did pour
The leperous distilment;
Ghost – *Hamlet*

Or have we eaten on the insane root
That takes the reason prisoner?
Banquo – *Macbeth*

1. HEMLOCK (*Conium maculatum*). Hemlock has had a sinister reputation for thousands of years, and is reputedly the plant that provided the death draught of Socrates. The Latin word *maculatum* means 'spotted', and any wild British plant that has purple-blotched leaves or stems is considered unfriendly, even if it is not actually poisonous.

2. YEW, HEBENON (*Taxus baccata*). Hebenon, hebona, heben and yew are deemed by the scholars to be different names for the same tree. Shakespeare uses both 'yew' and 'hebona', while contemporary authors such as Spenser and Marlowe prefer 'heben'.

3. INSANE ROOT (Henbane, *Hyoscyamus niger*). This is another Shakespearean name, which may have referred to any of the poisonous plants then known. Henbane is the most likely – it was formerly used by skilled herbalists as a (dangerous) sedative for the insane.

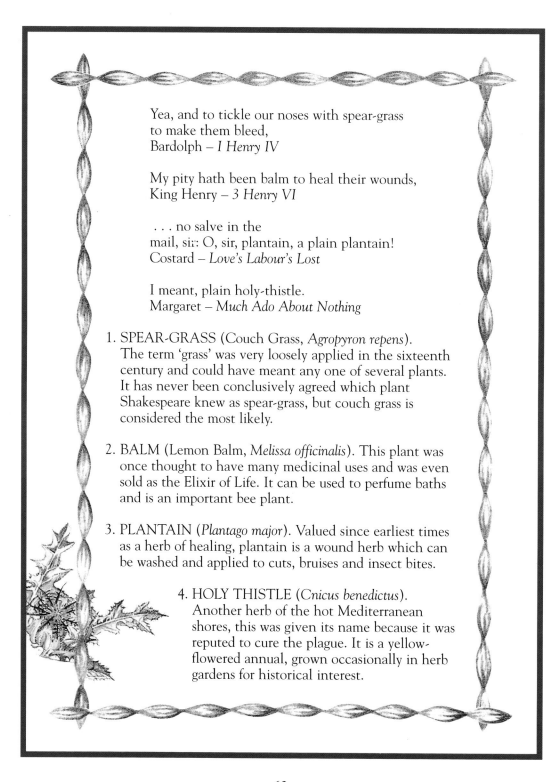

Yea, and to tickle our noses with spear-grass
to make them bleed,
Bardolph – *I Henry IV*

My pity hath been balm to heal their wounds,
King Henry – *3 Henry VI*

. . . no salve in the
mail, sir: O, sir, plantain, a plain plantain!
Costard – *Love's Labour's Lost*

I meant, plain holy-thistle.
Margaret – *Much Ado About Nothing*

1. SPEAR-GRASS (Couch Grass, *Agropyron repens*).
The term 'grass' was very loosely applied in the sixteenth
century and could have meant any one of several plants.
It has never been conclusively agreed which plant
Shakespeare knew as spear-grass, but couch grass is
considered the most likely.

2. BALM (Lemon Balm, *Melissa officinalis*). This plant was
once thought to have many medicinal uses and was even
sold as the Elixir of Life. It can be used to perfume baths
and is an important bee plant.

3. PLANTAIN (*Plantago major*). Valued since earliest times
as a herb of healing, plantain is a wound herb which can
be washed and applied to cuts, bruises and insect bites.

4. HOLY THISTLE (*Cnicus benedictus*).
Another herb of the hot Mediterranean
shores, this was given its name because it was
reputed to cure the plague. It is a yellow-
flowered annual, grown occasionally in herb
gardens for historical interest.

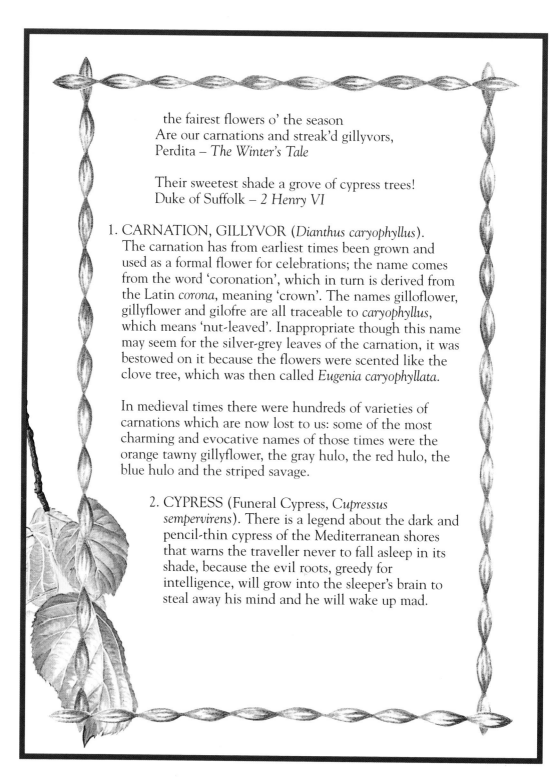

the fairest flowers o' the season
Are our carnations and streak'd gillyvors,
Perdita – *The Winter's Tale*

Their sweetest shade a grove of cypress trees!
Duke of Suffolk – *2 Henry VI*

1. CARNATION, GILLYVOR (*Dianthus caryophyllus*).
The carnation has from earliest times been grown and
used as a formal flower for celebrations; the name comes
from the word 'coronation', which in turn is derived from
the Latin *corona*, meaning 'crown'. The names gilloflower,
gillyflower and gilofre are all traceable to *caryophyllus*,
which means 'nut-leaved'. Inappropriate though this name
may seem for the silver-grey leaves of the carnation, it was
bestowed on it because the flowers were scented like the
clove tree, which was then called *Eugenia caryophyllata*.

In medieval times there were hundreds of varieties of
carnations which are now lost to us: some of the most
charming and evocative names of those times were the
orange tawny gillyflower, the gray hulo, the red hulo, the
blue hulo and the striped savage.

2. CYPRESS (Funeral Cypress, *Cupressus
sempervirens*). There is a legend about the dark and
pencil-thin cypress of the Mediterranean shores
that warns the traveller never to fall asleep in its
shade, because the evil roots, greedy for
intelligence, will grow into the sleeper's brain to
steal away his mind and he will wake up mad.

1

2

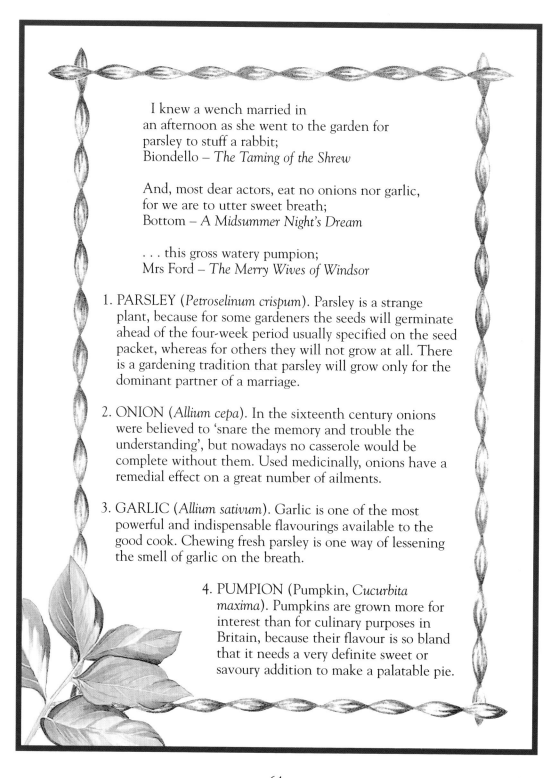

I knew a wench married in
an afternoon as she went to the garden for
parsley to stuff a rabbit;
Biondello – *The Taming of the Shrew*

And, most dear actors, eat no onions nor garlic,
for we are to utter sweet breath;
Bottom – *A Midsummer Night's Dream*

. . . this gross watery pumpion;
Mrs Ford – *The Merry Wives of Windsor*

1. PARSLEY (*Petroselinum crispum*). Parsley is a strange
   plant, because for some gardeners the seeds will germinate
   ahead of the four-week period usually specified on the seed
   packet, whereas for others they will not grow at all. There
   is a gardening tradition that parsley will grow only for the
   dominant partner of a marriage.

2. ONION (*Allium cepa*). In the sixteenth century onions
   were believed to 'snare the memory and trouble the
   understanding', but nowadays no casserole would be
   complete without them. Used medicinally, onions have a
   remedial effect on a great number of ailments.

3. GARLIC (*Allium sativum*). Garlic is one of the most
   powerful and indispensable flavourings available to the
   good cook. Chewing fresh parsley is one way of lessening
   the smell of garlic on the breath.

4. PUMPION (Pumpkin, *Cucurbita
   maxima*). Pumpkins are grown more for
   interest than for culinary purposes in
   Britain, because their flavour is so bland
   that it needs a very definite sweet or
   savoury addition to make a palatable pie.

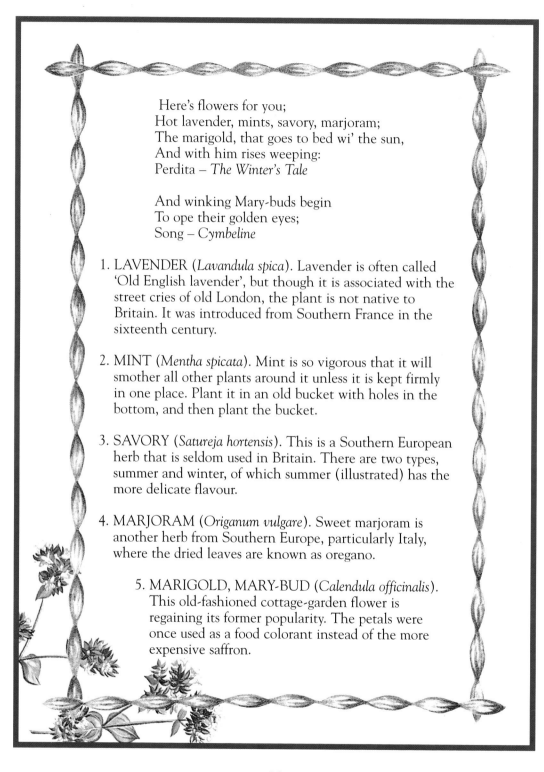

Here's flowers for you;
Hot lavender, mints, savory, marjoram;
The marigold, that goes to bed wi' the sun,
And with him rises weeping:
Perdita – *The Winter's Tale*

And winking Mary-buds begin
To ope their golden eyes;
Song – *Cymbeline*

1. LAVENDER (*Lavandula spica*). Lavender is often called 'Old English lavender', but though it is associated with the street cries of old London, the plant is not native to Britain. It was introduced from Southern France in the sixteenth century.

2. MINT (*Mentha spicata*). Mint is so vigorous that it will smother all other plants around it unless it is kept firmly in one place. Plant it in an old bucket with holes in the bottom, and then plant the bucket.

3. SAVORY (*Satureja hortensis*). This is a Southern European herb that is seldom used in Britain. There are two types, summer and winter, of which summer (illustrated) has the more delicate flavour.

4. MARJORAM (*Origanum vulgare*). Sweet marjoram is another herb from Southern Europe, particularly Italy, where the dried leaves are known as oregano.

5. MARIGOLD, MARY-BUD (*Calendula officinalis*). This old-fashioned cottage-garden flower is regaining its former popularity. The petals were once used as a food colorant instead of the more expensive saffron.

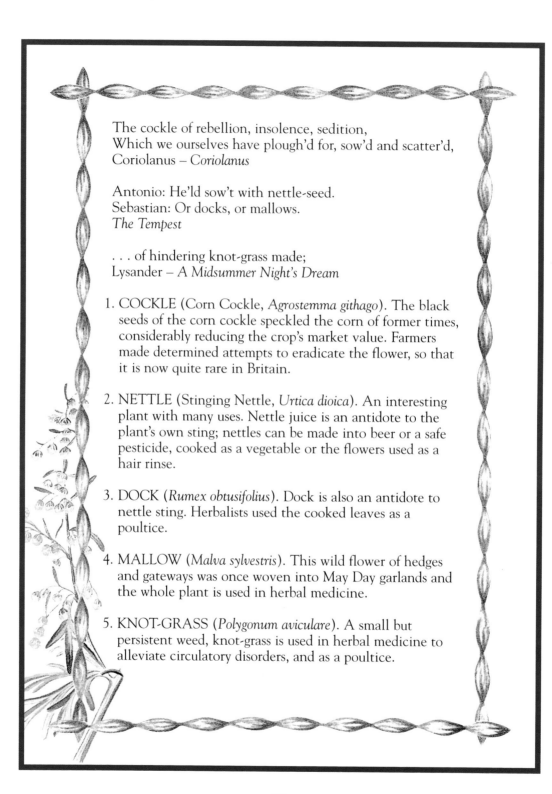

The cockle of rebellion, insolence, sedition,
Which we ourselves have plough'd for, sow'd and scatter'd,
Coriolanus – *Coriolanus*

Antonio: He'ld sow't with nettle-seed.
Sebastian: Or docks, or mallows.
The Tempest

. . . of hindering knot-grass made;
Lysander – *A Midsummer Night's Dream*

1. COCKLE (Corn Cockle, *Agrostemma githago*). The black
   seeds of the corn cockle speckled the corn of former times,
   considerably reducing the crop's market value. Farmers
   made determined attempts to eradicate the flower, so that
   it is now quite rare in Britain.

2. NETTLE (Stinging Nettle, *Urtica dioica*). An interesting
   plant with many uses. Nettle juice is an antidote to the
   plant's own sting; nettles can be made into beer or a safe
   pesticide, cooked as a vegetable or the flowers used as a
   hair rinse.

3. DOCK (*Rumex obtusifolius*). Dock is also an antidote to
   nettle sting. Herbalists used the cooked leaves as a
   poultice.

4. MALLOW (*Malva sylvestris*). This wild flower of hedges
   and gateways was once woven into May Day garlands and
   the whole plant is used in herbal medicine.

5. KNOT-GRASS (*Polygonum aviculare*). A small but
   persistent weed, knot-grass is used in herbal medicine to
   alleviate circulatory disorders, and as a poultice.

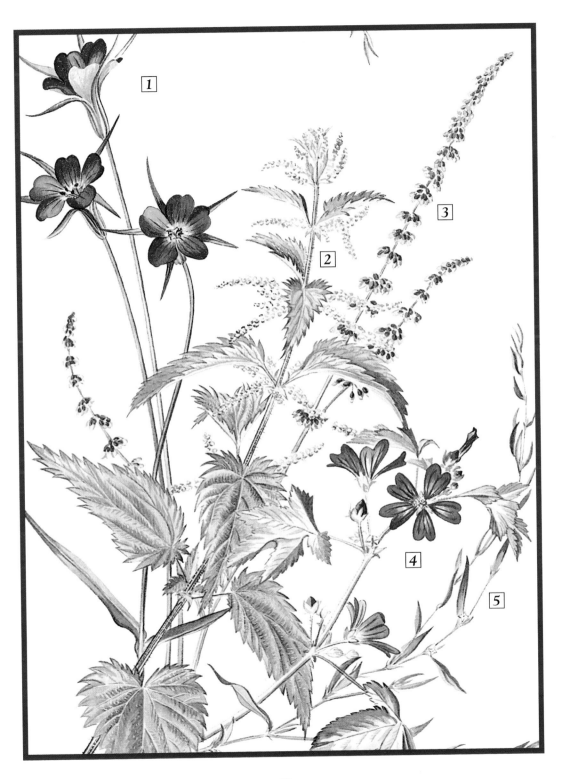

69

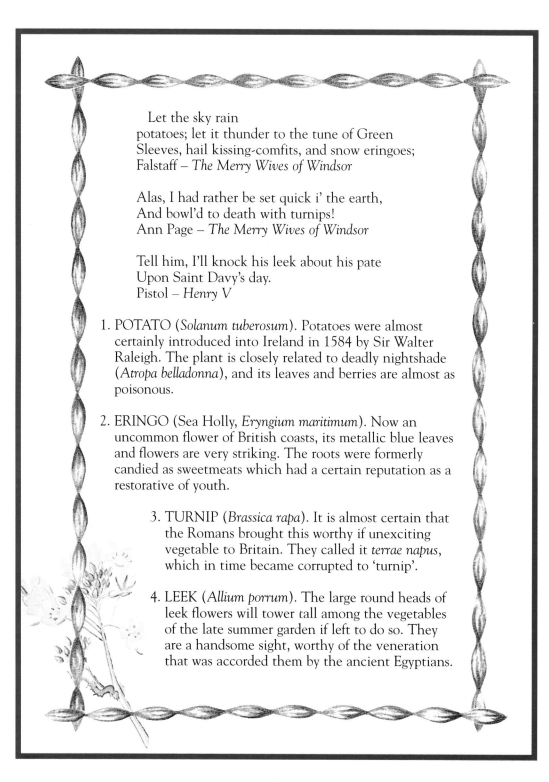

Let the sky rain
potatoes; let it thunder to the tune of Green
Sleeves, hail kissing-comfits, and snow eringoes;
Falstaff – *The Merry Wives of Windsor*

Alas, I had rather be set quick i' the earth,
And bowl'd to death with turnips!
Ann Page – *The Merry Wives of Windsor*

Tell him, I'll knock his leek about his pate
Upon Saint Davy's day.
Pistol – *Henry V*

1. POTATO (*Solanum tuberosum*). Potatoes were almost
   certainly introduced into Ireland in 1584 by Sir Walter
   Raleigh. The plant is closely related to deadly nightshade
   (*Atropa belladonna*), and its leaves and berries are almost as
   poisonous.

2. ERINGO (Sea Holly, *Eryngium maritimum*). Now an
   uncommon flower of British coasts, its metallic blue leaves
   and flowers are very striking. The roots were formerly
   candied as sweetmeats which had a certain reputation as a
   restorative of youth.

3. TURNIP (*Brassica rapa*). It is almost certain that
   the Romans brought this worthy if unexciting
   vegetable to Britain. They called it *terrae napus*,
   which in time became corrupted to 'turnip'.

4. LEEK (*Allium porrum*). The large round heads of
   leek flowers will tower tall among the vegetables
   of the late summer garden if left to do so. They
   are a handsome sight, worthy of the veneration
   that was accorded them by the ancient Egyptians.

71

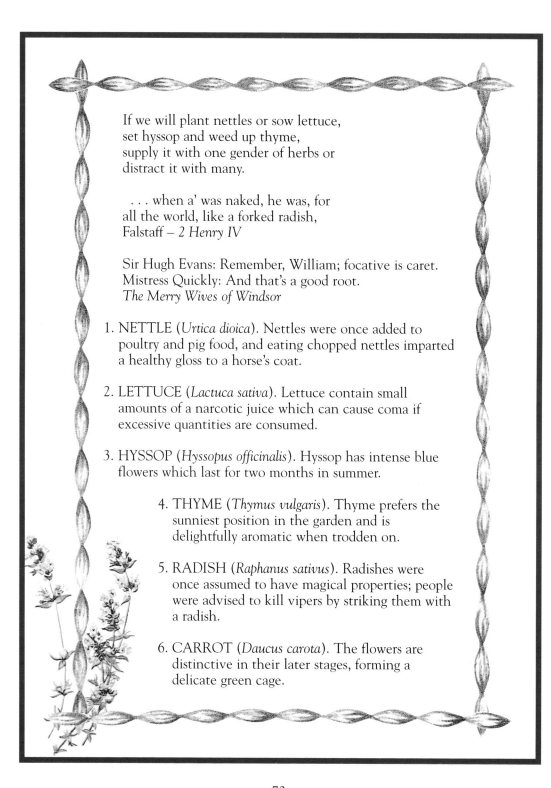

If we will plant nettles or sow lettuce,
set hyssop and weed up thyme,
supply it with one gender of herbs or
distract it with many.

. . . when a' was naked, he was, for
all the world, like a forked radish,
Falstaff – *2 Henry IV*

Sir Hugh Evans: Remember, William; focative is caret.
Mistress Quickly: And that's a good root.
The Merry Wives of Windsor

1. NETTLE (*Urtica dioica*). Nettles were once added to poultry and pig food, and eating chopped nettles imparted a healthy gloss to a horse's coat.

2. LETTUCE (*Lactuca sativa*). Lettuce contain small amounts of a narcotic juice which can cause coma if excessive quantities are consumed.

3. HYSSOP (*Hyssopus officinalis*). Hyssop has intense blue flowers which last for two months in summer.

4. THYME (*Thymus vulgaris*). Thyme prefers the sunniest position in the garden and is delightfully aromatic when trodden on.

5. RADISH (*Raphanus sativus*). Radishes were once assumed to have magical properties; people were advised to kill vipers by striking them with a radish.

6. CARROT (*Daucus carota*). The flowers are distinctive in their later stages, forming a delicate green cage.

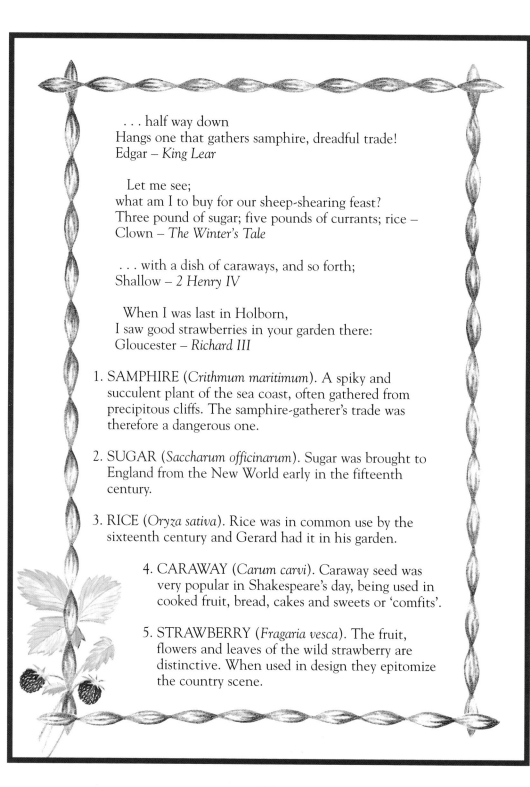

... half way down
Hangs one that gathers samphire, dreadful trade!
Edgar – *King Lear*

   Let me see;
what am I to buy for our sheep-shearing feast?
Three pound of sugar; five pounds of currants; rice –
Clown – *The Winter's Tale*

   ... with a dish of caraways, and so forth;
Shallow – *2 Henry IV*

   When I was last in Holborn,
I saw good strawberries in your garden there:
Gloucester – *Richard III*

1. SAMPHIRE (*Crithmum maritimum*). A spiky and succulent plant of the sea coast, often gathered from precipitous cliffs. The samphire-gatherer's trade was therefore a dangerous one.

2. SUGAR (*Saccharum officinarum*). Sugar was brought to England from the New World early in the fifteenth century.

3. RICE (*Oryza sativa*). Rice was in common use by the sixteenth century and Gerard had it in his garden.

4. CARAWAY (*Carum carvi*). Caraway seed was very popular in Shakespeare's day, being used in cooked fruit, bread, cakes and sweets or 'comfits'.

5. STRAWBERRY (*Fragaria vesca*). The fruit, flowers and leaves of the wild strawberry are distinctive. When used in design they epitomize the country scene.

And let the stinking elder, grief, untwine
His perishing root with the increasing vine!
Arviragus – *Cymbeline*

1. ELDER (*Sambucus nigra*). There was a time when nothing
good was ever said of an elder tree: it was evil-smelling, it
was unlucky to burn as firewood; it must not be used in
boat building or to make furniture; and Judas Iscariot was
reputed to have hanged himself from its branches.
However, at the same time it was believed that the elder
had the power to drive away evil spirits, because the tree
belonged to Hulda, the Scandinavian goddess of love. If
an elder tree grew in a garden, the owner would die
peacefully in his bed.

   Also on the credit side are the wind instruments that were
made from elder wood; the wines that can be made from
fruit and flowers; and many medicinal uses. Nevertheless
the elder is a sombre tree when not in flower, and nothing
else will grow in the shadow of its branches.

2. VINE (*Vitis vinifera*). The vine has been a solace to man
since earliest civilization, and very many books about
viticulture have been written in very many languages.
The Domesday Book lists 38 large vineyards in Britain –
yet another proof that our summers were warmer in
earlier times.

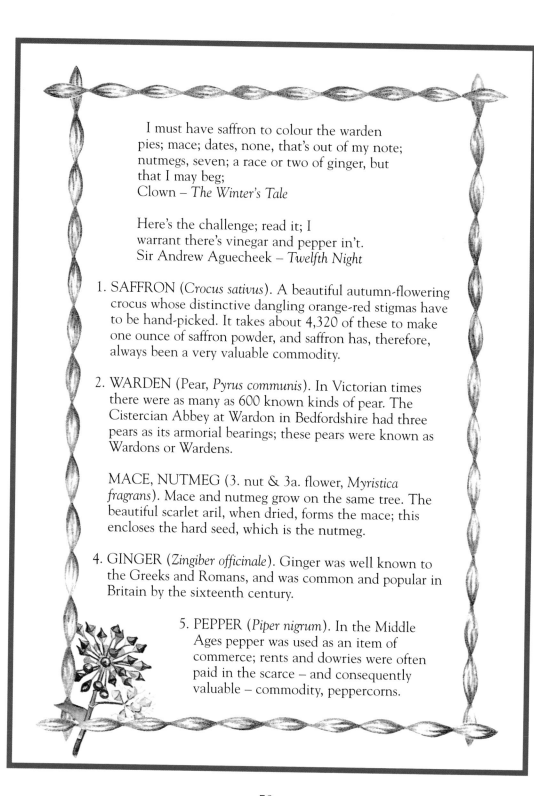

I must have saffron to colour the warden
pies; mace; dates, none, that's out of my note;
nutmegs, seven; a race or two of ginger, but
that I may beg;
Clown – *The Winter's Tale*

Here's the challenge; read it; I
warrant there's vinegar and pepper in't.
Sir Andrew Aguecheek – *Twelfth Night*

1. SAFFRON (*Crocus sativus*). A beautiful autumn-flowering
crocus whose distinctive dangling orange-red stigmas have
to be hand-picked. It takes about 4,320 of these to make
one ounce of saffron powder, and saffron has, therefore,
always been a very valuable commodity.

2. WARDEN (Pear, *Pyrus communis*). In Victorian times
there were as many as 600 known kinds of pear. The
Cistercian Abbey at Wardon in Bedfordshire had three
pears as its armorial bearings; these pears were known as
Wardons or Wardens.

MACE, NUTMEG (3. nut & 3a. flower, *Myristica
fragrans*). Mace and nutmeg grow on the same tree. The
beautiful scarlet aril, when dried, forms the mace; this
encloses the hard seed, which is the nutmeg.

4. GINGER (*Zingiber officinale*). Ginger was well known to
the Greeks and Romans, and was common and popular in
Britain by the sixteenth century.

5. PEPPER (*Piper nigrum*). In the Middle
Ages pepper was used as an item of
commerce; rents and dowries were often
paid in the scarce – and consequently
valuable – commodity, peppercorns.

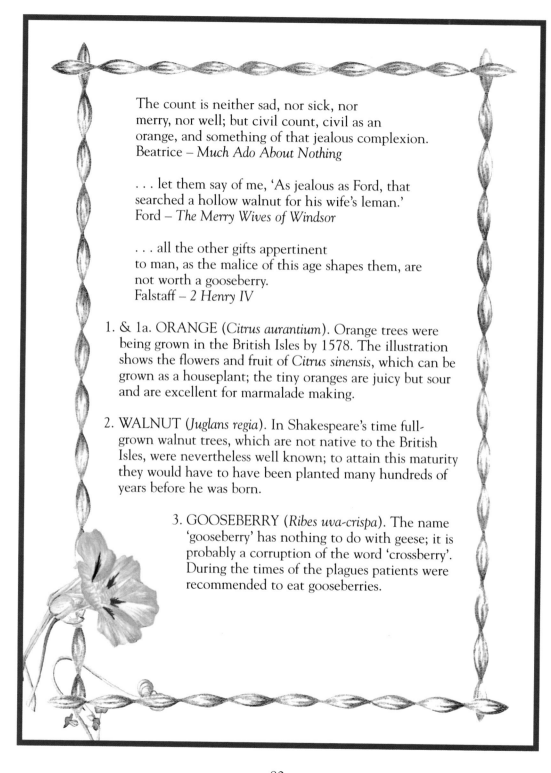

The count is neither sad, nor sick, nor
merry, nor well; but civil count, civil as an
orange, and something of that jealous complexion.
Beatrice – *Much Ado About Nothing*

. . . let them say of me, 'As jealous as Ford, that
searched a hollow walnut for his wife's leman.'
Ford – *The Merry Wives of Windsor*

. . . all the other gifts appertinent
to man, as the malice of this age shapes them, are
not worth a gooseberry.
Falstaff – *2 Henry IV*

1. & 1a. ORANGE (*Citrus aurantium*). Orange trees were
being grown in the British Isles by 1578. The illustration
shows the flowers and fruit of *Citrus sinensis*, which can be
grown as a houseplant; the tiny oranges are juicy but sour
and are excellent for marmalade making.

2. WALNUT (*Juglans regia*). In Shakespeare's time full-
grown walnut trees, which are not native to the British
Isles, were nevertheless well known; to attain this maturity
they would have to have been planted many hundreds of
years before he was born.

3. GOOSEBERRY (*Ribes uva-crispa*). The name
'gooseberry' has nothing to do with geese; it is
probably a corruption of the word 'crossberry'.
During the times of the plagues patients were
recommended to eat gooseberries.

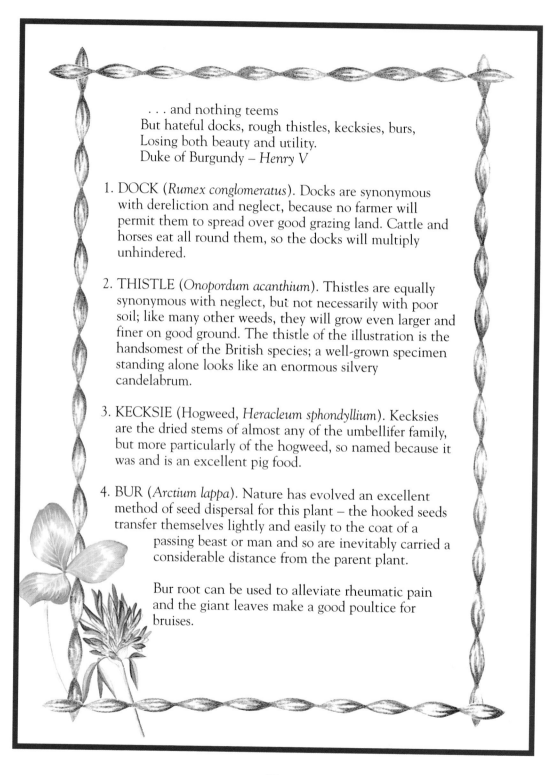

> . . . and nothing teems
> But hateful docks, rough thistles, kecksies, burs,
> Losing both beauty and utility.
> Duke of Burgundy – *Henry V*

1. DOCK (*Rumex conglomeratus*). Docks are synonymous with dereliction and neglect, because no farmer will permit them to spread over good grazing land. Cattle and horses eat all round them, so the docks will multiply unhindered.

2. THISTLE (*Onopordum acanthium*). Thistles are equally synonymous with neglect, but not necessarily with poor soil; like many other weeds, they will grow even larger and finer on good ground. The thistle of the illustration is the handsomest of the British species; a well-grown specimen standing alone looks like an enormous silvery candelabrum.

3. KECKSIE (Hogweed, *Heracleum sphondyllium*). Kecksies are the dried stems of almost any of the umbellifer family, but more particularly of the hogweed, so named because it was and is an excellent pig food.

4. BUR (*Arctium lappa*). Nature has evolved an excellent method of seed dispersal for this plant – the hooked seeds transfer themselves lightly and easily to the coat of a passing beast or man and so are inevitably carried a considerable distance from the parent plant.

   Bur root can be used to alleviate rheumatic pain and the giant leaves make a good poultice for bruises.

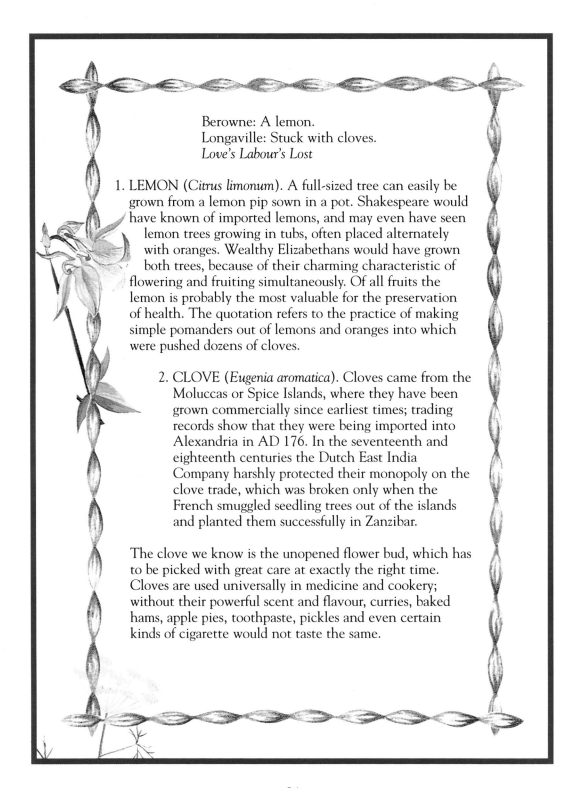

Berowne: A lemon.
Longaville: Stuck with cloves.
Love's Labour's Lost

1. LEMON (*Citrus limonum*). A full-sized tree can easily be grown from a lemon pip sown in a pot. Shakespeare would have known of imported lemons, and may even have seen lemon trees growing in tubs, often placed alternately with oranges. Wealthy Elizabethans would have grown both trees, because of their charming characteristic of flowering and fruiting simultaneously. Of all fruits the lemon is probably the most valuable for the preservation of health. The quotation refers to the practice of making simple pomanders out of lemons and oranges into which were pushed dozens of cloves.

2. CLOVE (*Eugenia aromatica*). Cloves came from the Moluccas or Spice Islands, where they have been grown commercially since earliest times; trading records show that they were being imported into Alexandria in AD 176. In the seventeenth and eighteenth centuries the Dutch East India Company harshly protected their monopoly on the clove trade, which was broken only when the French smuggled seedling trees out of the islands and planted them successfully in Zanzibar.

The clove we know is the unopened flower bud, which has to be picked with great care at exactly the right time. Cloves are used universally in medicine and cookery; without their powerful scent and flavour, curries, baked hams, apple pies, toothpaste, pickles and even certain kinds of cigarette would not taste the same.

Angelica   Dramatis persona, *Romeo and Juliet*

If seasons were as
plentiful as blackberries, I would give no
man a reason upon compulsion, I.
Falstaff – *1 Henry IV*

1. ANGELICA (*Angelica archangelica*). A stately plant with a stately name, angelica differs from its multitudinous relatives in having a completely spherical umbel of flowers. It was once considered to bestow good luck in the spring and was carried ceremonially in European 'Maying' processions. The plant was also believed to cure the plague and is thought to have been named after the Archangel Michael, whose day is 8 May. Before 1732 angelica would have been in flower in early May; since the alteration to the calendar in that year, it now blooms at the end of the month or in early June.

2. BLACKBERRY (*Rubus fruticosus*). The bramble or blackberry is mentioned in the Old Testament Book of Judges in the parable of the trees who wished to choose a king of their own kind to reign over them. The olive, the fig and the vine all refused the honour for various selfish reasons, and the humble bramble was elected king.

   When picking blackberries it is useful to remember that the crushed leaves possess styptic properties and a simple poultice may be applied to the unavoidable scratches. Legend has it that blackberries should not be picked after Michaelmas (29 September), because the Devil defiles the fruit by spitting on it – or worse.

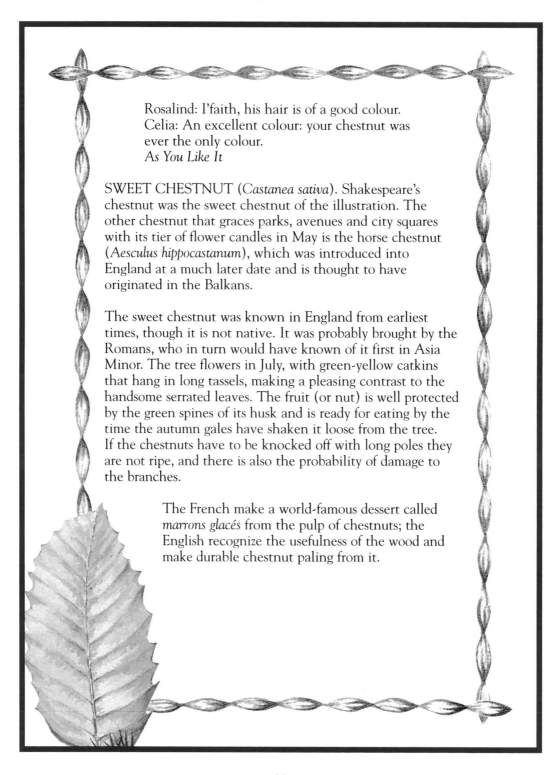

Rosalind: I'faith, his hair is of a good colour.
Celia: An excellent colour: your chestnut was
ever the only colour.
As You Like It

SWEET CHESTNUT (*Castanea sativa*). Shakespeare's
chestnut was the sweet chestnut of the illustration. The
other chestnut that graces parks, avenues and city squares
with its tier of flower candles in May is the horse chestnut
(*Aesculus hippocastanum*), which was introduced into
England at a much later date and is thought to have
originated in the Balkans.

The sweet chestnut was known in England from earliest
times, though it is not native. It was probably brought by the
Romans, who in turn would have known of it first in Asia
Minor. The tree flowers in July, with green-yellow catkins
that hang in long tassels, making a pleasing contrast to the
handsome serrated leaves. The fruit (or nut) is well protected
by the green spines of its husk and is ready for eating by the
time the autumn gales have shaken it loose from the tree.
If the chestnuts have to be knocked off with long poles they
are not ripe, and there is also the probability of damage to
the branches.

The French make a world-famous dessert called
marrons glacés from the pulp of chestnuts; the
English recognize the usefulness of the wood and
make durable chestnut paling from it.

Now would I give a thousand furlongs of sea for
an acre of barren ground, long heath, brown
furze, any thing.
Gonzalo – *The Tempest*

There is a man. . .
hangs odes upon hawthorns and elegies on brambles;
Rosalind – *As You Like It*

The oaks bear mast, the briars scarlet hips:
Timon – *Timon of Athens*

1. HEATH (*Erica tetralix*). It is not certain whether
Shakespeare meant a flower at all here. The 'long heath'
may well have been a stretch of desolate moorland.

2. FURZE (Gorse, *Ulex europaeus*). 'Kissing's out of season
when the gorse is out of bloom' runs the old saying –
because gorse is always in flower somewhere.

3. HAWTHORN (*Crataegus monogyna*). The red and gold of
the leaves and the subdued crimson of the berries bring a
brief glow to the sombre late autumn hedgerow.

4. BRAMBLE (*Rubus fruticosus*). By Shakespeare's time
the word 'bramble' had come to mean only the
blackberry.

5. OAK (*Quercus robur*). Hogs were formerly
fattened up on all the woodland nuts, which
had the generic title of 'mast'. The term is now
only used for 'beech mast'.

6. BRIAR (*Rosa canina*). Here Shakespeare
means the fruit of the wild rose, but 'bramble'
and 'briar' formerly signified any thorny plant.

O'ercome with moss and baleful mistletoe:
Tamora – *Titus Andronicus*

Heigh-ho! sing heigh-ho! unto the green holly:
Amiens – *As You Like It*

If aught possess thee from me, it is dross,
Usurping ivy, brier, or idle moss;
Adriana – *Comedy of Errors*

1. MOSS (*Thuidium tamariscinum*). Mosses have many forms and colours; this particularly bright green species grows on damp ground, on trees and on rotting wood.

2. MISTLETOE (*Viscum album*). Mistletoe is a strange parasitic plant, full of legend and mystery. It has always been associated with the druids and is therefore seldom used in church decoration at Christmas.

3. HOLLY (*Ilex aquifolium*). It is considered lucky to have a holly growing near the house. Male and female plants are borne on separate trees and holly should always be planted in small groups which include both sexes.

4. IVY (*Hedera helix*). The ivy's flowers are among the last of the year, and on warm days in late autumn the ivy bushes hum with the activity of the feeding insects.

5. BRIAR (*Rubus fruticosus* & spp). To compensate for the wicked thorns of the mature briar, there is the summer harvest of beautiful and delicious fruit. The plants supply larval food and nectar for several rare species of butterfly.